GHOSTS OF THE YADKIN VALLEY

Ghosts of the Yadkin Valley

R.G. ABSHER

Haunted America

Published by Haunted America
A Division of The History Press
Charleston, SC 29403
www.historypress.net

All images by the author unless otherwise noted.

First published 2009

Manufactured in the United States

ISBN 978.1.59629.711.1

Library of Congress Cataloging-in-Publication Data

Absher, R. G.
Ghosts of the Yadkin Valley / R.G. Absher.
p. cm.
ISBN 978-1-59629-711-1
1. Ghosts--North Carolina--Yadkin River Valley. I. Title.
BF1472.U6A27 2009
133.109756'6--dc22
2009015723

To my mom Helen Absher, "Ma Helen," for her loving guidance and support through the years.

CONTENTS

PREFACE

The first time I heard really exciting ghost stories was in my youth in the early 1970s. I was a youngster growing up in the town of Taylorsville, North Carolina. It was late in summer. The night noises of the crickets, singing bugs, tree frogs and distant cars accompanied the sounds of a crackling campfire. These were carefree August nights. The evening stars came out as friends, neighborhood kids and even neighborhood dogs sat around the campfire. Tales and ghost stories were sometimes exchanged into the wee hours of thc night. A neighbor, Leonard Gant, would catch the unsuspecting off guard during the midst of a scary story by sneaking up behind him and touching a straw behind the ear of the victim. This prank almost universally caused the subject to jump into the air, resulting in a successful prank and the familiar laughter from Mr. Gant.

Around those campfires, I would learn and retell those stories that have fueled a lifelong interest in ghosts and shadowy tales. For years I have traveled around the tourist areas, historic towns and sites, and have been a frequent participant on as many ghost tours as I could muster. From these years of being a "ghost tour sampler," I have learned a lot of strange and fascinating tales in the process. I've also noted many common threads that make these sites and haunts both compelling and mystifying.

In my twenty-five-plus years of residing in the Yadkin Valley of North Carolina, I have been employed with the U.S. Army Corps of Engineers as a park ranger at W. Kerr Scott Reservoir. Years of hanging around many of the folk of the region have resulted in the accumulation of a wealth of tales and stories. I guess that by being around the music scene as well as the historic community, it is expected that I might have run into a lot of odd stories and odd characters too! In my spare time, I collected these stories, sometimes as a matter of fact and sometimes as a matter of conscience.

During the last several years, I've really picked up the pace in my ghost chase. I visited the sites of the stories and then researched the historical information surrounding them. The ghost research and search, if you will, has resulted in some very good finds. I've discovered fascinating accounts, often finding remarkable historical clues backing up the stories. I've also interviewed lots of people. Perhaps this has been the most enjoyable aspect of the process. I must admit that at times during interviews, I felt like I was some kind of psychological advisor or a paranormal talk show host. Wow, in spite of all the unusual conversations and interviews, it was worth it! After all, I talked to real live people who have witnessed firsthand some very strange and unexplained happenings.

The sense of awe and mystery from these collected accounts has inspired me to write this book. Although I do invite the reader to ponder the obvious question, "Do you believe in ghosts?" it is not my attempt in this book to convince anyone that ghosts exist. My main focus is to let these stories roll, to intertwine them with historical details of area and place and then to let your imagination run as it may.

It is my goal that the reader will become more aware of the rich history of this place, which has a culture nearly bigger than life. Wilkes County at one time went all the way to the Mississippi River and is still referred as the Great State of Wilkes. Technically, Wilkes County could have included the greater portion of Tennessee. But for the scope of this book, I have pinpointed the region of present-day Wilkes and the surrounding counties along the Yadkin River Valley. I hope that by adding a "sprinkling of history," I will whet your appetite to discover more. Along with the history, hopefully you will enjoy the stories, leaving the door open for the possibilities.

Preface

The great writer Alfred Hitchcock often left the door open for "the possibility." It's the thought of "the possibility" that makes these stories interesting and causes the imagination to drift into another time and place where events almost freeze in time. It is my wish that you will encounter a few passages that will spark or excite deep intrigue in that regard. I hope that I challenge you to tap into your imagination and your sense of wonder. This is what storytellers have been shooting for since the settlement of America.

From the Salem witch trials of New England to the misty fields of Gettysburg, Pennsylvania, ghost stories are a part of American history. From Charleston and Savannah to Colonial Williamsburg, and the back roads of Appalachia, ghost stories have slipped into our culture all the way back to the colonial period. The information contained in this book will examine the stories along the upper Yadkin Valley communities in Western North Carolina.

And what a historic area it is! The names and happenings of the region are the stuff of familiar legends in American folklore. In this lush green valley, the citizens endured two major military campaigns, including the campaign to the Battle of Kings Mountain in the Revolutionary War and Stoneman's Raid in the War Between the States. In one sentence, you can say Daniel Boone, Tom Dooley and even NASCAR! In the heyday of moonshining, it became "necessary" to build fast cars to outrun the law. The cars and the driving skills of men in the hills became legendary. NASCAR racing legend Junior Johnson and many others became experts at building high-performance engines for cars that could outrun the government-issued standard patrol cars of the day. Movies such as *Thunder Road* were produced about this legendary practice of running white liquor. These bootlegger stories could fill volumes.

And what once was shine country is now wine country. For those interested in the Yadkin Valley as a wine destination, see the reference link in the area attractions section in the back of the book. In an hour drive from my home in Elkin, I can reach over thirty vineyards.

Rising from the economic hardships created by two world wars and the Great Depression, the industrious and innovative citizens of the rural backcountry along the upper Yadkin River rose to create national businesses in poultry and home improvement industries. Today, Tyson Foods and Lowes Home Improvement Warehouse are pretty much household names on the lips of thousands of Americans.

So welcome to one of the most historic regions of North Carolina. In reading some of these ghastly tales, I sincerely hope that you gain a greater appreciation of the history as well. It has been a desire of mine to make sure that our rich history is not forgotten. I have a keen interest in telling the stories and promoting our heritage tourism assets along our towns and communities in the valley.

All the drama and intensity of the region over time have yielded a treasure chest of stories of the weird and scary along with the awe-inspiring and historic. Regarding the ghost tales, I encourage you to ponder the details of these stories and then make your own evaluation as to "the possibilities." I also encourage you to visit some of the sites mentioned here and to enjoy their historic side as well. It will then be up to you to determine for yourself, "Could this really be…?"

A Ghost Tour Is Born

In 2003, I embarked with a group of citizens to complete a major renovation of the 1902 Old Wilkes County Courthouse, which stands in downtown Wilkesboro. The Wilkes Heritage Museum ribbon cutting took place on November 15, 2004. As I looked around me on the steps of the Old Wilkes County Courthouse that day, I stood with a team of folks who had made the Heritage Museum project possible. A relatively small board and group of dedicated volunteers put together a successful business plan and fundraising campaign. The result is a magnificent facility that will promote and preserve history for present and future generations.

Having the opportunity to travel in Europe on a number of occasions, and to visit many historic sites in America, over time I have developed a love of historic buildings and places. I've strolled the streets of Savannah, Wilmington and Williamsburg and have noted that all of these places do a wonderful job of promoting tourism through their candlelight ghost walks. After taking these tours over several years in other historic towns, I began to investigate the possibility of doing ghost tours in historic Wilkesboro, North Carolina. During the winter of 2004–05, I started a venture to set up the Wilkes Heritage Museum Candlelight Ghost Tours in downtown Wilkesboro. In the process of doing the ghost research, it became apparent that quality ghost stories were both prevalent and numerous. My list of ghost stories quickly grew. Within six months, I had accumulated a large file of tales and stories.

Another discovery was that public interest in ghost tours was high. On the historic night of July 3, 2005, its very first evening, the Candlelight Ghost Tours drew over three hundred people. Folks showed up to take the tours, which were conducted under the light of candle lanterns by our guides in colonial dress under the light of candle lanterns. The first ghost tours visited the haunts of the Old Wilkes Jail, Smithey's Hotel and the Wilkesboro Town Cemetery. From those inaugural tours, it soon occurred to me that folks were interested in this part of our folk heritage. At that point, I decided to write this book. When the muse of inspiration spoke and friends urged me on, I decided to proceed. I threw my hat over the fence and followed after it!

The local press, the *Winston Salem Journal*, *NC UNC Public TV*, *Welcome to Wilkes* magazine and *Images of Wilkes* magazine, has covered our ghost tours. Someone even called me from the Dominican Republic asking for the stories. So I invited him to visit and take the ghost tour. Since then, other area authors have published books of stories from the lower Yadkin area. My focus here is primarily the upper Yadkin Valley of North Carolina, which is quickly becoming a wine and heritage tourism destination. Thank you for purchasing this book. I hope that you truly enjoy the stories contained within and that you will retell them and inspire others to share the art and fun found in storytelling. In addition, I also invite you to visit the Wilkes Heritage Museum, take in the ghost tour and join us in efforts to promote and preserve history for future generations. Now let us see if we can dig up some ghosts and voices of the past!

ACKNOWLEDGEMENTS

Chapter 1
Jeremiah Greer
Shadows in the Dark, host
www.shadowsinthedarkradio.com
"Where Darkness Is Illuminated"
jgreer@shadowsinthedarkradio.com
828.400.0836

Chapters 3, 5, 8 and historic site notes and photos
Wilkes Heritage Museum
100 East Main Street
P.O. Box 935
Wilkesboro, NC 28697
www.wilkesheritagemuseum.com
336.667.3171

Chapter 3, part 2
Kenneth W. Robinson
Director of Public Archaeology
Wake Forest University
Winston-Salem, North Carolina

Chapter 3, part 3
Ron Harris
Bethlehem, NC

Chapter 4
Lyman C. Draper
Kings Mountain and Its Heroes, 1881

Chapter 4, William Lenoir
Becky Phillips
Fort Defiance
Lenoir, NC
828.758.1671
www.fortdefiancenc.org

Chapter 5, General Gordon's historical notes
Chris J. Hartley
Stuart's Tarheels, James B. Gordon and His North Carolina Calvary, 1996

Chapter 6
Court Records of the Trial of Tom Dooley
NC Court Achieves, Raleigh, NC
Wilkes Heritage Museum (same as above)
Interviews and site field visits with Edith Marie Carter and Karen Wheeling Reynolds
Words to "Tom Dooley," Doc Watson Version

Chapter 7
Dr. R. Ernest Cohn
308 East Main Street
Wilkesboro, NC 28697
www.holisticmedclinic.com

Chapter 8, Benton Hall and photos from *Tom Dooley, a Wilkes County Legend*
Karen Wheeling Reynolds
Wilkes Playmakers

300 D Street
North Wilkesboro, NC 28659
www.wilkesplaymakers.com
336.838.7529

Yadkin Valley Attractions
Linda Check
Wilkes Chamber of Commerce
717 Main Street
North Wilkesboro, NC 28659
336.838.8662
www.WilkesNC.org
www.ExploreWilkes.com

Additional Acknowledgements
Wilkes Heritage Museum: Jennifer Furr, Terry Lutar, Diana Perry and Marilyn Payne
Wilkes Community College Library: Dr. Fay Byrd, Misty Bass, Vickie Cothren and Cristy Earp

Chapters 8 and 9
The ghost guides/storytellers of the Wilkes Heritage Museum
Julie Mullis, Eric Payne, Dub Canter, Heather Osborne, Dr. Charles Gilreath, Adam Furr, Sandra Watts, Chip Furr, Edith Marie Carter and Krista Trivette
Wilkes Community College Southern Culture Class: Julie Mullis and the students who assisted in collecting ghost stories

The ghost interviews: Harold Bass, Carol Black, Dub Canter, Edith Marie Carter, George Childers, Guy Church, Dr. R. Ernest Cohn, Sue Cohn, Seth Cohn, Tammy Dinardo, Chip Furr, Angela Gambill, Dr. Charles Gilreath, Larry Green, Terrian Green, Mark Green, Mickey Minton, Matt Minton, Julie Mullis, April Nichols, Heather Osborne, Mr. and Mrs. Bobby Phillips, Allison Phillips, Eric Payne, Marilyn Payne, Karen Reynolds, Jory Shepherd and the students of the Southern Culture Class at Wilkes Community College

Acknowledgements

Photos/Portraits: William Vance Nichols, Karen Reynolds, Donna Absher, Marilyn Payne, Terry Lutar, Jennifer Furr, Dr. R. Ernest Cohn, Wilkes Community College and the Wilkes Heritage Museum

CHAPTER 1

CLASSIC HAUNTED HOUSE CHARACTERISTICS

From England and Ireland to Savannah and Williamsburg, I've found that ghost places share historically related themes and have strong ties to their historical past. In addition, these sites have witnessed a range of human emotions. Whether it's a Civil War battlefield in America or the Tower of London in the United Kingdom, violent events, gruesome tragedies and subsequent ghost legends abound. What I have discovered in my ghost quest of the Yadkin Valley is that the stories here also have a common thread of emotional trauma and other human emotions that connect to their histories. Many of these haunted sites and houses share patterns or characteristics in the stories that emerge from them.

In order to more fully enjoy the stories that follow, I thought it would be good to address at the beginning of this book what constitutes some of the classic haunted house characteristics and unexplained supernatural ghost experiences. Then, as you read through the stories that follow, hopefully some similarities and patterns of these characteristics will begin to emerge. For example, I've found that descriptions of occurrences from English castles often mirror those of American buildings. Paranormal happenings at battlefields in Europe are similar to those reported at American battlefields, and similarities are often found among haunted houses.

Another thing about ghost encounters is that they may not be limited by boundaries of time and space. Although late-night encounters in spooky settings are the most noticed, most celebrated and offer the paranormal investigators the most distraction-free environment, occurrences can take place in any location or at any time of day. In addition, ghosts don't discriminate against gender, social status or ethnicity. Virtually anyone can experience the strange and unexplained. Of special interest are the same basic descriptions of ghost encounters told independently by different persons. In the stories that follow, a fair amount of them also involve these "independent sightings."

Ghost experiences are not as rare as one might think. People are often reluctant to admit or report such encounters for obvious reasons. I've discovered, however, that it is not unusual to have at least one or more folks on my ghost tours who can tell of an explained or suspected paranormal event in their lives. I've been surprised that, when asked, a good percentage of people can tell you about something unexplained that happened to them at some point in their journey. There must be some reason why people are drawn to ghost stories. Before we dive into the stories, let's examine a few of the things to watch for.

One of the most common haunted house characteristics that people report are all kinds of sounds. Some common sounds include footsteps on staircases or people walking in adjacent rooms or other floors. Many people are convinced that the sounds could not be caused by anything but another person. People insist that they are not caused by the "mouse in the attic" or by the "bird flying through windows." Some descriptions are very specific, such as "running children," "men walking in heel taps" or "people locked in an eternal struggle."

Yet another type of occurrence is the sound of human voices. Descriptions range from normal talking to moaning, crying and laughter. Again, folks say that the voices are not caused by moving rafters, winds or rain noise but are like real live human voices. Often no environmental conditions exist that could have caused the sounds. The weird variant of the human voice is the description of demonic or chant-like tones. Sometimes these demonic variants include hysterical laughter, moaning, echoing or even wailing siren voices that rise and fall in pitch. The voices may sound distorted, have alien-like qualities or sound like they are in foreign or unknown languages. Imagine just for a moment that you are alone and in a spooky setting and suddenly hear a strange, troubling voice that you only thought possible in a horror movie.

Moving objects are commonly experienced. Examples include moving furniture, slamming or creaking doors, rocking chairs, missing or moving silverware and china, interacting portraits and hovering, floating or flying objects. I've had more than one person say that they've observed objects move or hover during a Ouija board game or a séance.

Smells of the familiar or the nostalgic are often encountered in haunted houses. Smells of foods cooking or characteristic smells like pipe smoke, desserts, etc., are sometimes mentioned. Some relate old smells that they encountered in their childhood. People have reported visiting houses of someone who they knew and sensing smells of familiar recipes that they remember from thirty years ago when granny was cooking for a holiday meal.

A few years ago, my wife and I took a ghost tour in Wilmington. When we were walking around a corner and listening to the tour guide tell the strange tales of a house, my wife and I noted, almost simultaneously, the very distinct smells of cured tobacco. The tour guide, who was totally unaware of our experience, told us a few minutes later that sometimes people smelled tobacco in this area of the tour.

This type of experience leads me to discuss perhaps the most interesting ghost experience of all—the actual sighting of what appears as a flesh and blood human being. Very bizarre and weird descriptions usually go with these kinds of sightings. Sometimes people report hearing a voice or witnessing an unexpected view or apparition of a person from another time or point in history. Some have visited famous battlefields and thought they saw soldiers or even regiments from a historic battle. Some report seeing people drifting through walls or vanishing in a vapor. As in the accounts in the Smithey's Hotel in downtown Wilkesboro, sightings connect with historic figures who lived in the house. This type of sighting is called a "historical association." Paranormal investigators tell us that historical association makes for some of the most interesting sites. Some such stories are found in the pages ahead.

Ghost hunters often place ghost sightings in two categories —residual or interactive. Residual sightings are those that replay an event or experience at the same building or site. This is almost like an image, sound or pattern of activity that repeats itself over and over and is witnessed a number of times, often by different people. These type of experiences behave as if captured on a self-continuous loop, like a stuck recording.

Interactive ghost experiences are described as those in which the ghost appears to be aware of the person witnessing the event. The person may experience a sensation of a presence or the feeling of being watched. Reports of a "presence" often involve a zone within a structure, site or building. These interactive sightings or encounters are sometimes considered annoying or frightening. In the interactive ghost experience, the ghost seems to react by moving objects, responding to questions, causing havoc, creating sensations of being touched or altering the mental disposition of the subject. This type of experience is the frequent focus of infamous poltergeist movies.

Both residual and interactive hauntings are reported in many of the stories in this book. In addition, some experiences involve the five senses and some even appear to read the mind of the subject! These reported "sixth-sense" ghost happenings are bizarre and even remarkable.

So here we go. Let's look at the curious and the unusual. Let's examine some of the first-person accounts and experiences that happened to people who passed on these stories. And if you know of any stories yourself, I would like to hear them!

R.G. Absher
160 Brenhaven Drive
Elkin, NC 28621
336.902.1760
absher-r@juno.com

CHAPTER 2

SÉANCE ON THE MOUNTAIN

My interest in ghost stories goes back to my youth in Alexander County, North Carolina. I was loading up with the other kids from my high school English department on a Halloween night in the early 1970s. The number of students and teachers combined totaled ninety-plus people. I recall that the weather that evening started off very clear and beautiful. Farm tractors and trailers were lined up at the Alexander Central High School parking lot ready to embark to the top of Barrett's Mountain for the Halloween party that followed.

The scene was very picturesque, as hay wagons filled with laughing teens made their way outside the city limits of Taylorsville, North Carolina, and continued along a few rural roads. Along the way, fall wildflowers were brilliantly displayed along the roadsides. Deeply yellow goldenrod and purplish Joe Pye weed displayed their fall plumage. The fall leaves were nearly at their full-blown, multicolored peak. The rugged countryside and farms were beautifully adorned with pumpkins and haystacks laying in fields. The smells of dry hay and the burned fall leaves were vividly imprinted in my memory. The sounds of a few scattered guitars and banjos could be heard between the voices of kids and the rumble of the tractor engine as we rode along the route. The thirty-minute ride from the school to the top of Barrett's Mountain soon concluded along a dusty dirt road, but the kids never seemed to mind breathing in a little dust. The laughing and cheering students rode on to the top of the mountain. It was a carefree and delightful early evening and it hardly seemed that anything unusual would disturb the fun and gaiety of the hayride to Barrett's Mountain.

I remember that someone mentioned that Barrett's Mountain was known to be haunted and that being up on that mountain on Halloween would increase the chances of paranormal activity. When this was suggested, a chorus of skeptical laughter quickly followed the comment. When we arrived at the top of the mountain, the evening campfires had already been started and the food was quickly brought out for the weenie roast to follow. Soon after the cookout and mass marshmallow roast, the attention turned to the subject of ghost stories, tales and spooky subjects. Finally, after a round or so of stories, many of which were whimsical in nature, a few really quality stories were told. Some of the students obviously had grown up around some of the good storytellers of the area.

After we exhausted most of the ghost stories, the idea of holding a séance emerged from the group. Discussion quickly shifted to who was to lead the séance. Who in the group would have the necessary qualifications to lead the task? Finally, the teacher, Ms. Little, asked the group, "Okay, we need someone from our class who is uninhibited, someone with some acting skills to lead the séance…I believe we need someone who is just a little off the wall, somebody with magnetism, and with a big loud projecting voice! Okay, which one of my students in this class can really make this feel like a real honest to goodness classic séance?" Almost universally, every kid present that night instinctively pointed directly at me. Well at least it didn't take long for the class to decide. I was usually the first person to volunteer! I suddenly was preparing myself to do something that I had never attempted. Even if it was all in fun, it still gave me a cold chill that I was about to lead ninety-plus classmates and people gathered on Barrett's Mountain on this beautiful harvest night in a séance! I gathered up a little strength and then fired back to the group, "Okay, I'll do it!"

As the group gathered around the huge campfire, the circle seemed almost magical. I did some quick work and quickly shot from the hip, deciding to ham up the endeavor and draw off my early 1970s ringleader reputation to arrive at the role of being leader of the séance. As it turned out, what seemed like child's play and fun began a night that I will never forget.

A makeshift costume was quickly made for me. From a red picnic tablecloth, a turban was made and wrapped around my head. Some other kids placed a long raincoat over my back in imitation of a cape or cloak. As the kids completed their last-minute touches in applying my costume, I thought to myself, "I might at least play this thing up a little and get some good laughs out of the event." So here I go!

I had the group of ninety-plus sit in a circle and join hands. Off we ventured into a realm that I have never before or after experienced. At first the group wished to call up everybody from former local officials and businesspeople to schoolteachers who were deceased. Somebody even suggested calling up the town drunk! Following the whimsical remarks and pokes of fun, the séance finally got serious. After a brief discussion, the group unanimously decided to call up some of the ex-presidents of the United States.

I noticed that just before we started, the weather was calm and the skies were filled with stars. There were no clouds in sight. However, after I began asking questions and attempting to communicate with the afterlife, something very strange and unexplained happened. Suddenly, the winds picked up and moaned through the surrounding treetops. Then, a loud crash of thunder followed with a severe downpour of rain. This was such a dramatic change that practically all the youngsters were terrified. Chaos followed!

Teachers suddenly went into command mode. They ordered all the students to board the wagons for the return ride to the high school. They gathered up the picnic baskets and wind-tossed flying objects and secured them into the hay wagons as they hurried students into place. It was scary, especially to all of the students caught in the frightening storm. During the ride down the mountain, one of the students had a panic attack, and upon arrival at the school, received treatment from the medics who had been dispatched to the scene. Many students fell into a state of pandemonium. Later, they remarked that I must have been the troublemaker responsible for the madness. Regardless of the how or why for the strange turn of events, almost all present that night felt like we had ventured into an area where we shouldn't have gone. Whether the event was caused by some unexplained power, I can say that it was my first and last séance.

For many years to follow, when former classmates ran into me somewhere in public or at a high school class reunion, they would hold up two fingers outstretched and make a "protective cross" as if to ward off evil. Other people would always ask me, "Hey, what's with the cross thing, man?" I would relate the story. I would tell them the account of the very strange experience that took place on Barrett's Mountain that Halloween night. I was not the only one to remember. Ninety-plus students and teachers witnessed an unexplained occurrence following that hayride to Barrett's Mountain. On that night, I was the leader of the séance on the mountain.

CHAPTER 3

GHOSTS OF THE COLONIAL PERIOD

NATIVE AMERICAN OCCUPATION

Some have cited possible reasons for the abundance of haunts in the Yadkin Valley. The valley has witnessed many struggles, conflicts and violence throughout its history. Yet another reason cited is the presence of Native American burial and ceremonial grounds. Like the lands of the famous bell witch haunting in Tennessee, several sections of the upper Yadkin Valley were once ancient burial grounds. One thing's for sure, the area of present-day Wilkesboro and many other locations along the Yadkin Valley were occupied by Native Americans long before the colonial period. For centuries, the Native Americans fished in the waters of the Yadkin and hunted the nearby forests for game. In addition, they farmed the fertile flood plain, growing corn, beans and squash. Those early Americans also used the higher sections of bottomlands and surrounding hills for mystical ceremonies and for the burial of their dead.

Virtually every major period of Indian prehistory is represented by artifacts found in the Yadkin Valley. Based on spear points, arrow points and other stone artifacts, Native Americans were in the Yadkin Valley as far back as eight thousand years. It is evident from archaeology that the eastern woodland and Mississippian period mound builders were the predecessors of the Cherokee, and thrived in large numbers as far back as AD 500. During the colonial period, the activities of the Cherokee and Catawba were most often

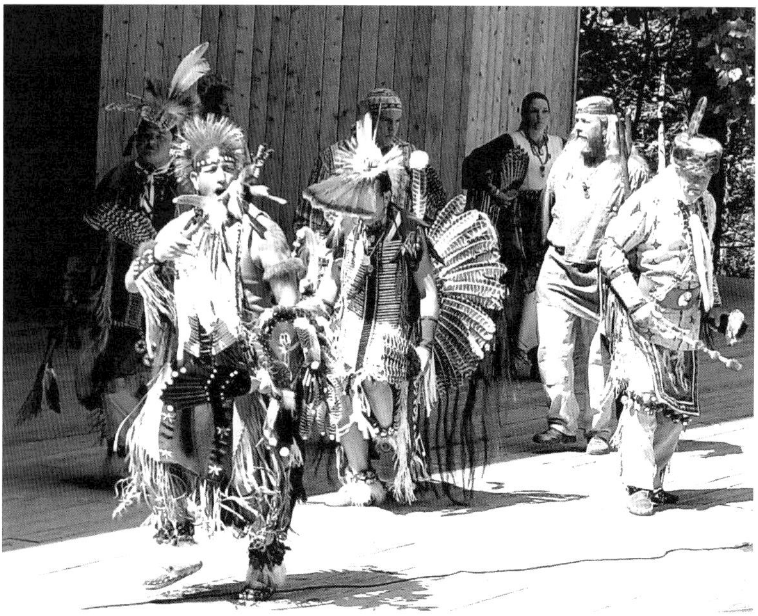

An annual Native American powwow held at Kerr Scott Lake in the Yadkin Valley.

acknowledged by early explorers and settlers of the region. Today, many folks from Western North Carolina, including me, have some Cherokee ancestry in their family lineage.

In 2008, I made a trip to Bethlehem, North Carolina, to the home of Ron Harris, a very well-known and nationally respected collector of Native American artifacts. I was there to video for the "Save Our History" oral history project for Wilkes County. After I observed his vast collection of artifacts and interviewed him with extensive questions about the Native American occupation of the region, it was apparent that Wilkes and surrounding counties were heavily populated by Native Americans during the centuries leading up to settlement from Europeans. Ron has frequently advised the curators of Wilkes Heritage Museum and the staff of W. Kerr Scott Reservoir on the dates of artifacts that have been found along the Yadkin Valley. He showed me examples of intricate and finely crafted spear points dating back more than eight thousand years.

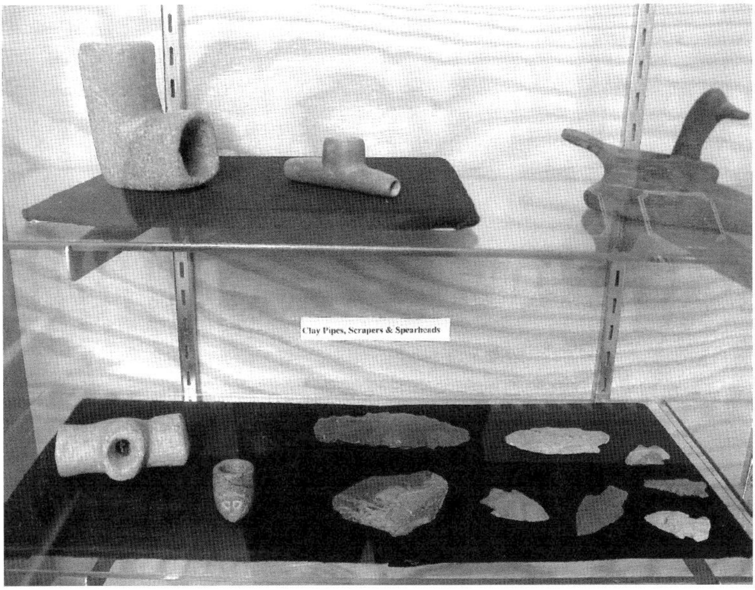

Yadkin Valley Native American artifacts at the Wilkes Heritage Museum.

In 1883, Dr. J.M. Spainhour, a Lenoir dentist and expert on Indian customs, contacted the Smithsonian Institution and enlisted the help of a team, led by J.P. Rogan, to assist in conducting archaeological studies in the upper Yadkin Valley in the area near Patterson known as Happy Valley. Finds included many skeletons, pottery and fragments, projectile points, stone gaming disks, stone axes and ceremonial objects. This early work confirmed a strong woodland period occupation in the upper Yadkin Valley. Since those early days of archaeology, other digs conducted in the Yadkin Valley have further confirmed Native American occupation along the upper Yadkin Counties. An unnamed Native American mound can still be viewed in Caldwell County just across the road from Patterson School along NC Highway 268 in Patterson.

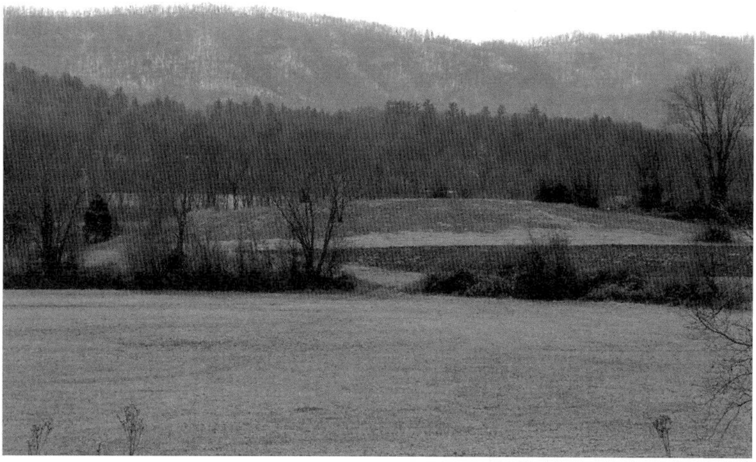

A Native American mound near Patterson School along the upper Yadkin Valley in Caldwell County.

MULBERRY FIELDS

In downtown Wilkesboro, one can stand near the location of St. Paul's Episcopal Church and look down into the valley where a large Cherokee village once stood. In 1752, after receiving a commission from the Earl of Granville, Bishop August Gottlieb Spangenberg, superintendent of Moravian missions and settlements, set out to survey a tract of 100,000 acres that included the upper Yadkin Valley and a large region of the surrounding area of northwest North Carolina. During late fall, Spangenberg found a large Indian village in the area now described as the bottomland along the present-day towns of Wilkesboro and North Wilkesboro. Apparently, the Cherokee were engaging in a large gathering, perhaps the annual corn harvest ceremony, or "busk." Indications are that several hundred thatched-roof houses were noted in the bottomland at the time.

The Cherokee word *Keowee* means "Mulberry Grove" or "Mulberry Fields." It is presumed that the Moravians gave the old village site the name Mulberry Fields in acknowledgement of Spangenberg's observation. Mulberry Fields stood as its name until the town of Wilkesboro was laid out in 1800 by William Lenoir.

Painter William Nichols made trips to Cherokee, North Carolina, to research the period of the 1750s Native American villages. After consulting with historic documents and with eighteenth-century Cherokee traditions, Nichols painted a large representation of the Cherokee village at Mulberry Fields. The painting now hangs in the Wilkes Heritage Museum. The Cherokee are depicted as they might have been discovered by Bishop Spangenberg and his survey party back in 1752.

As for the theory of the burial ground haunts, it was Cherokee practice at that time to bury their dead in the surrounding high grounds above the flood plains just outside the village. So it is likely that downtown Wilkesboro today is the location of ancient burial

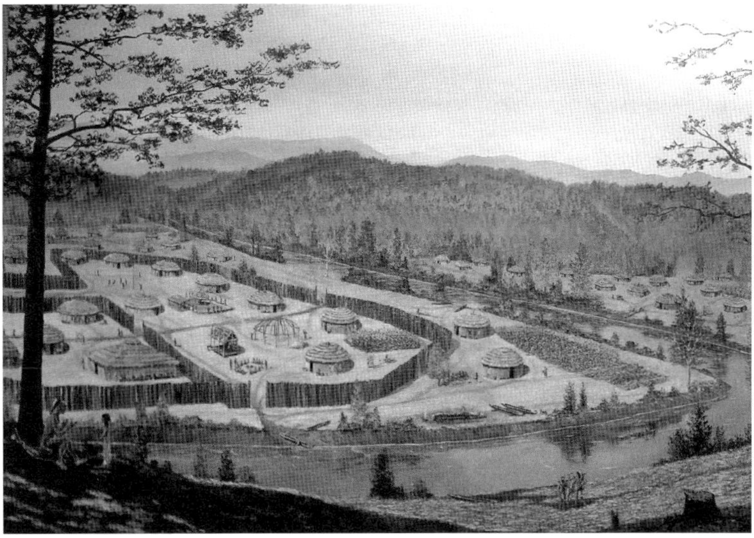

The 1752 Cherokee village of Keowee as interpreted by painter William Vance Nichols. *Courtesy of the Wilkes Heritage Museum.*

grounds. This fact adds to the interest among those who study ghostly tales and the paranormal.

TALE OF TWIN POPLARS

Late on a warm spring day in 1991, three whitewater kayakers emerged from their car on an old abandoned dirt road at a place near NC Highway 321 just north of Lenoir, North Carolina. My kayaking buddies James Eller and Whit Arnold and I had just run the waterfalls in Wilson Gorge, a large boulder-filled creek in Pisgah National Forest, which is located deep in the lush hills of Burke County, North Carolina. After enjoying a beautiful ride down the river, I told the guys about an intriguing side trip to a site known as the Twin Poplars. After talking James and Whit into interrupting our car ride back to Wilkes County, we pulled off the road and took a trail that coursed along a shimmering, mountain-fed creek.

After a short hike along the stream, we found the subject of our interest. Twin Poplars, a massive tree or pair of tree trunks that merged into one tree about twenty feet above the ground, reached upward about 120 feet in total height. Very mysterious indeed! Whit and James were very impressed. Although nothing happened in a paranormal sense on our visit, my two kayaking buddies did inquire about the legend of Twin Poplars.

It turns out that the twin poplar tree has been recognized by people for many generations as having an enchanted past connected to a violent event that took place at the site, which was called Warrior's Gap back in 1737. In that year at the site, a battle of massive scale took place between the Cherokee and the Catawba Indians, who were in a major dispute over the territory. Although the traditional dividing line or boundary "Eswau Huppeday" between Cherokee and Catawba lands was located southwest of the area, the region near the divide of the Catawba and Yadkin River watersheds was heavily disputed. Warrior's Gap was the site of the massive historic battle between the Cherokee and Catawba Nations, perhaps the largest land battle ever to take place between two Native American tribes.

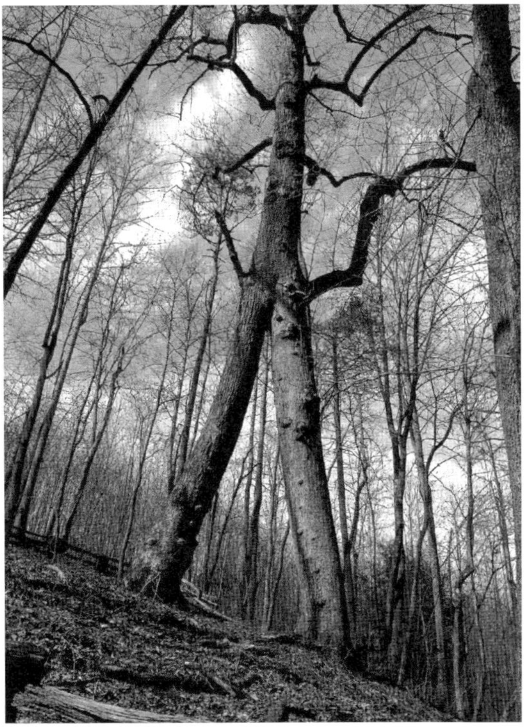

The Twin Poplars, a living symbol of peace between the Cherokee and Catawba Nations.

During this period, only a scattering of Scotch-Irish had migrated into the area, so they were not the direct cause of the battle. However, increased competition for land and territory may have made the Indians agitated by their presence. Interestingly, the battle account and what followed was retained in both Cherokee and Catawba traditions. Several thousand braves from each side came to Warrior's Gap, located on a feeder creek of the Yadkin River, and fought a battle that lasted for several days at the site. The terrible battle caused a great loss of life. The Cherokee and Catawba evidently locked into a bloody stalemate with neither side gaining an advantage.

Finally, the two sides agreed to stop the fighting and two poplar saplings were tied together to symbolize peace. The two trees still stand today and can be spotted along the small path known as Twin Poplars trail. The tale, however, does not end there, but is connected with the haunting and perplexing story of the Brown Mountain Lights.

CONNECTIONS TO THE BROWN MOUNTAIN LIGHTS

From several views along the Linville Gorge rim, for generations, people have spotted the Brown Mountain Lights. The lights sometimes appear deep in the canyon or gorge and then fade, float or appear to move about as ghostly spotlights. The number of lights varies from one to several at a time. From some vantage points, only the top of the long mountain ridge is visible. From these views, the lights seem to appear on the top edge of the ridge and then slowly move upward and hover. They sometimes pulsate, often brilliantly, sometimes changing colors and sometimes blinking on and off. The lights typically last several minutes before disappearing. Then, after a few minutes, the same sequence of events may occur again. The cause of these mysterious lights has remained a mystery for decades but they were visible to the Native Americans even before the settlers began noticing the Brown Mountain Lights. Several popular theories have been suggested but none proven.

A legend that has persisted since colonial days is about the great Native American battle that took place at Warrior's Gap in 1737. Following the great battle, the Cherokee maidens supposedly left their villages to hunt for their lost warriors. The battle site was just a few miles from Linville Gorge. The maidens became lost and wandered into the deep and remote gorge wilderness near Brown Mountain. Legend says that their torch lights are still visible on cold clear nights. As grieving Indian maidens continue to look for their long lost braves, the torch lights yet appear.

> *High over yonder and down in the canyon at below, It shines like the crown of angels, and fades as the mists come and go.*
> *—chorus from song "The Brown Mountain Lights," by Scotty Wiseman*

CHAPTER 4

THE AMERICAN REVOLUTIONARY WAR

For many years, a mighty oak tree stood as a symbol of American independence in downtown Wilkesboro. The Tory Oak, as it was called, stood for perhaps over three hundred years—that is, until nature began to take its course. The aging tree was finally felled by a series of intense thunderstorms in the early 1990s. The Tory Oak, the place of public execution, symbolized the struggle for freedom and independence and the beginning of the United States of America. As in other famed execution sites around the world, much mystery and intrigue surrounds the Tory Oak site.

A few years before the tree fell, during a historic celebration of the Tory Oak history, I stood with descendants of both the British Loyalists who were hanged there and the descendants of the executioner, Colonel Ben Cleveland. These folks had come together to exchange their thoughts on what had happened. These were interesting conversations to say the least. I must say that they all came away with a heightened appreciation for what the site represented in history.

In eastern Wilkes County, the lazy Yadkin River, which once was known as "Roundabout," makes a huge horseshoe-shaped bend. The large track of bottomland was once the home of Colonel Benjamin Cleveland, Patriot leader in the Southern Campaign of the Revolutionary War. A creek that now enters the former landholdings of Colonel Cleveland is today called Bugaboo Creek. The area has a reputation for being haunted, mostly from the story relating to Colonel Ben's adventures in the Revolutionary War.

Benjamin "Ben" Cleveland was born in 1738 near Bull Run Creek near present-day Manassas, Virginia, and in 1769, he moved to the Yadkin River to the area of Ronda known then as "Roundabout," which was in the bend of the Yadkin River. Today the land is the Chatham farm. Cleveland had a fondness for such gatherings as horse races and community muster events of the militia. He loved hunting, fiddling and strong drink. Ben Cleveland cared not much for routine farming work.

When the American Revolution broke out, Cleveland served as colonel of the Wilkes County Militia and was one of the major leaders at the Battle of Kings Mountain. Cleveland was a massive man, weighing well over three hundred pounds. He was notoriously tough on the British Tories during the American Revolutionary War. He was a blunt man and dealt harshly with those siding with the British cause during this bitter period of civil conflict.

Numerous accounts of Cleveland's hangings of the British Tories can be found in Lyman Drapers's *Kings Mountain and Its Heroes*, which was written in 1881, the 101st anniversary of the Battle of Kings Mountain. We will discuss Cleveland's hangings in more depth later, but for now we will focus on Colonel Benjamin's actions at the Battle of Kings Mountain and the story of the ghost of Bugaboo Creek.

THE GHOST OF BUGABOO CREEK

Following the fall of Charleston in the spring of 1780, the American Patriot cause in the Revolution against the mother country was looking bleak. The British government had shifted its strategy to the southern colonies in an effort to turn back the Patriot movement. The plan was to recruit American Loyalists to fight against American Patriots. The plan appeared to be working. The Americans lost a decisive battle in Camden, South Carolina, in August 1780 when General Horatio Gates took an ill-prepared army hastily into battle against the well-trained and rested British army under General Charles Cornwallis. The loss at Camden was considered the worst American defeat in the Revolutionary War and, for a short time, eroded support for the Patriot side. Fortunately, however, one pocket of resistance did remain in the Carolinas in the late summer of 1780. That resistance continued in the backcountry settlements along river valleys and over the mountains of present-day Virginia, Tennessee, North and South Carolina and Georgia.

These mountain men, or backwater men, as they were called, were rough, independent and sturdy folk. They had learned the hard lessons from a generation of Indian fighting, hunting from the forest and farming under difficult conditions. They carved their independence through hard work and determination. "Ever-ready to Hug a Bear," or fight for a cause threatening their freedom, they trusted in God and kept their powder dry.

Lord Cornwallis, aware of this rebel stronghold, was ready to take action. The British militia leader was Major Patrick Ferguson, born in Scotland. Ferguson was the inventor of an early breechloading rifle (most were loaded from the muzzle in the eighteenth century), and was an able leader in the British army. Ferguson was rumored to have passed up an opportunity to shoot General George Washington at the Battle of Brandywine because Washington was in an unfair position at the time. Washington was talking to his men around the campfire and was not engaged in battle. Patrick Ferguson, who was well trained in the art and etiquette of war, passed up the opportunity that would have changed the course of history.

Major Patrick Ferguson was in charge of the left flank of Cornwallis's army, which was positioned near present-day Charlotte, North Carolina. Lord Cornwallis had tasked Ferguson to "subdue the patriot resistance in that quarter of North Carolina." Ferguson, with his notorious campaigning skills, was busy enlisting support for the royal standard. Ferguson recruited Loyalist Americans to serve and fight against the Patriot Americans.

It was Ferguson's aggressive behavior that also led to his demise. He reached a location just a few miles above present-day Rutherfordton, North Carolina, at Gilbert Town, where he delivered his famous ultimatum. Ferguson sent a message to the overmountain forces that said, "If ye do not desist opposition to British Arms, I will march my army over the mountains, hang your

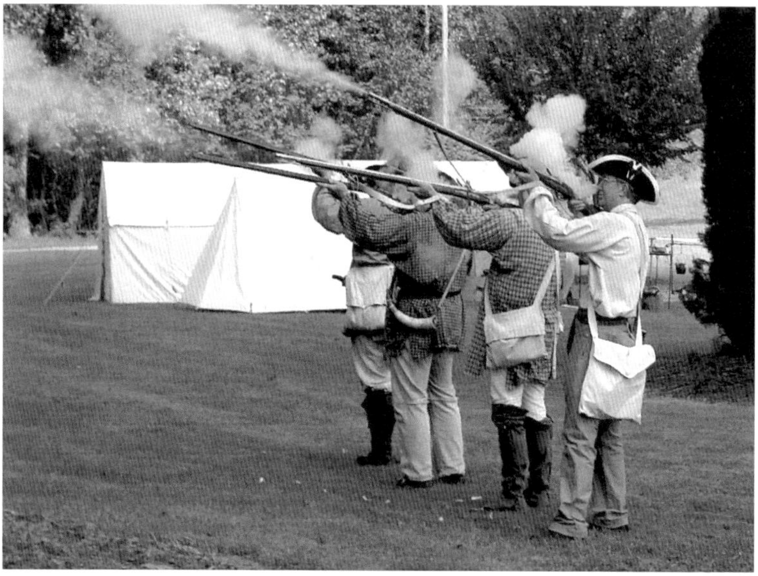

Overmountain Victory Trail Association reenactors fire guns at the site of the muster grounds.

leaders and lay waste to your countryside with fire and sword!" It did not take long for this dispatch to reach the population, and the response was dramatic. Patriot militia forces, armed with primarily the Pennsylvania hunting rifles, left the safety of their farms and mountain homes and formed an all-volunteer army to go after Ferguson and his Loyalist militia.

This overmountain militia came from over the hill settlements of the Watauga, Holston, Nolichucky and New River Valleys and from settlements below the mountains, including the Yadkin and Catawba River Valleys. In all, the militia force of over 1,200 men came from present-day eastern Tennessee, southwest Virginia, North and South Carolina and Georgia. Just a few days later, the overmountain forces finally reached Gilbert Town to find that Ferguson had vanished.

It was at Gilbert Town that Colonel Benjamin Cleveland helped turn the pages of history by urging that the Overmountain Men continue the chase for Ferguson and catch him before he could return to the safety of Lord Cornwallis in Charlotte. Patriot leaders then assembled the overmountain forces together and Cleveland entered the circle of men and made a stunning and emotional speech: "I have come to tell you the news. It is time for each of us to up and at them!" Cleveland and Isaac Shelby, another key Patriot colonel, essentially talked the Patriot militia force into continuing the chase of Ferguson.

Ferguson's Loyalist force was caught on October 7 in South Carolina near the North Carolina border on a low mountain crest known as Kings Mountain. In a hotly contested battle lasting around one hour, rugged mountain men dressed in homespun clothing and armed with long rifles succeeded in winning the day from the bayonet-charging Tory force directed by Ferguson. Ferguson had made a bold statement saying, "This is Kings Mountain, and I am King of the mountain…and even God almighty cannot dislodge me from this mountain."

Ferguson's prophesy proved true. Following several failed charges of the Loyalist force under Ferguson, the long rifles of the attacking Patriots began to show signs of attrition. But the Tories, armed with bayonet and smoothbore guns, proved ineffective given the lay of

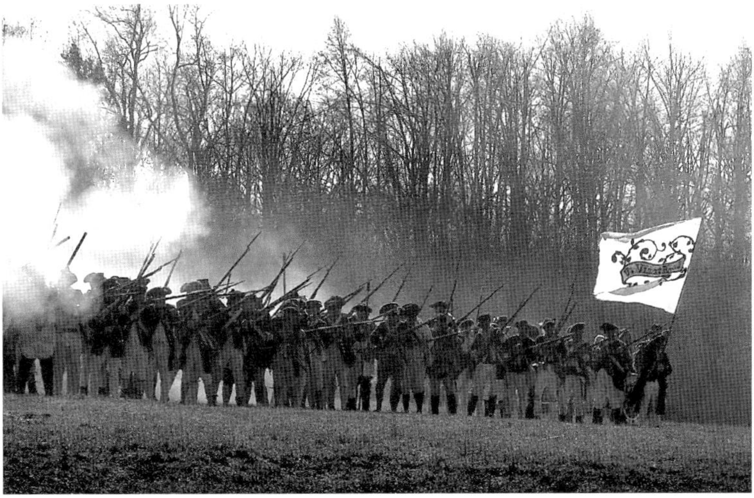

A Revolutionary War reenactment battle scene.

land and the heavily forested surroundings. The cover of the trees and brush played to the advantage of the Patriot force. Amidst the thunder of rifles and heavy smoke and cries of wounded and dying men, the battle reached a turning point. After realizing the day was lost, Ferguson, with his sword flashing in hand and his silver whistle blasting commands, attempted to charge the Patriot lines. He was riddled with at least eight round balls and fell from his white horse and died. He is buried in a Scottish cairn just a few feet from where he fell.

The Loyalist units were squeezed into a small bald area on one end of the footprint-shaped mountain ridge. The British Tories began to cry for quarter. It took a few minutes for the American forces to stop shooting into the surrendering Loyalist troops. The Loyalists were forced to surrender.

Colonel Benjamin Cleveland's men had been instrumental in stopping the final Loyalist resistance and they had fought gallantly during the battle. Cleveland was described by some as moving about his men, urging them to fight on and "be your own officer." At Kings Mountain, Cleveland was a giant of a leader.

For his bravery in leading the Wilkes Militia in the Battle of Kings Mountain, Colonel Benjamin Cleveland was presented with the prized animal that had belonged to Major Patrick Ferguson. Cleveland's horse, Roebuck, had been shot out from under him during the battle and he was overjoyed to obtain the beautiful white steed. The white Arabian horse was of "Royal horse ancestry" and was as well known and celebrated as any horse that existed in the entire British army during the American Revolution.

A few weeks after, Colonel Benjamin returned to the Roundabout with the prized Arabian horse. For years, people would ride by the plantation and remark on the beauty of the white horse that once had belonged to Patrick Ferguson. The horse became a favorite of the community. It was only when the animal died that a fantastic tale emerged.

For years, and even up to present times, people report seeing a strange white horse with a red-coated rider carrying a sword and galloping along the river bottoms along the old Roundabout Plantation at the confluence of Bugaboo Creek and the Yadkin

River. To this day, people riding through the area along NC Highway 268 complain that their cellphones routinely go out when they cross Bugaboo Creek.

The White Horse Ghost

Colonel Ben was his name, from the Yadkin he came, a leader and a Patriot by fame.
Rasseled bears they did say, drank rum and played, and he fought like the Celts of yore.
Old roundabout twas great, at his largest did weigh, 300 good pounds or more.
But before judgment day, they all heard him say, he would hang British Tories eve' more.

In the summer of seventeen and eighty, came a message weighty, came a call from the Tory Left,
Cornwallis at Charlotte, sent a Scot after the heart, of men sharing Cleveland's good deft.
A call then came, dispatch riders they say, of Ferguson, from Gilbert Town afar,
If Ye Do Not Desist, and bow to good King George, "I'll lay waste with fire and sword."

On a pale moon night, spy the white horse light, see the ghost of bug-a-boo creek.
Ferguson's checkered shirt, and his sword held high, He rides again to seek.
When Ferguson charged, he did fall and his horse did get away.
At Liberties call, his horse did fall into Cleveland's hands that day.
Col. Ben brought him back to his Rhonda farm, where the white horse ghost still plays.

The call then rang, from the mountains so far, the militia then gathered so fast.
On September twenty five, to the Watauga they came, to a place on Sycamore Flats.
From valley's Holston to Doe, New River and Toe, to put an end to the Tories at last.
Women stayed home, to defend alone, the danger of Indian attacks.

The roaring Doe they crossed the Roan they marched, and then up the Yellow Mountain Gap.
With Sevier, from Nolichucky, and Shelby and Campbell, from a tough stock were sturdy as tack.
Uniforms they lacked, but with trusty rifles they came, with backbones as tough as a knot.
They saddled their horses, appealed to the almighty, and made off to give chase in a trot.

On a pale moon night, spy the white horse light, see the ghost of bug-a-boo creek.
Ferguson's checkered shirt, and his sword held high, He rides again to seek.
When Ferguson charged, he did fall and his horse did get away.
At Liberties call, his horse did fall into Cleveland's hands that day.
Col. Ben brought him back to his Rhonda farm, where the white horse ghost still plays.

They met Colonel Ben, at Quaker that day, down on the Catawba River Fields.
To Gilbert Town they sped, Fergie had fled, where'd the fox go, we shall see.
Ben Cleveland drew a line, in the sand that day, and shouted for liberty.
Back out or fight, you now must decide—Who will stay and fight with me?

The American Revolutionary War

They caught him October 7, Cornwallis had no chance, at Kings Mountain in Caroline,
Patrick Ferguson was surrounded, Bayonets in the sky, Tory green was cornered in time.
Yelling boys from hills high, carried sharper shooters to nigh, captured a hill on Sat-ur-day.
When Ferguson Charged, he did fall, and his horse did get away.

On a pale moon night, spy the white horse light, see the ghost of bug-a-boo creek.
Ferguson's checkered shirt, and his sword held high, he rides again to seek.
When Ferguson charged, he did fall and his horse did get away.
At Liberties call, his horse did fall into Cleveland's hands that day.
Col. Ben brought him back to his Rhonda farm, where the white horse ghost still plays.

Mountain men on the hill, their voices were shrilled, as they yelled in the art of the Celts.
Come fight with me, for liberty to see, if we banish this hill for the free.
Shout like devils from ore, and I'll show you some more, of the Tories dead on the hill.
For their cause is yet bad, for they know not our plan, to make a country of freedom for man.

Silver whistle in hand, Ferguson waving commands, his sword did flash in the sky.
The sharpshooters nigh, had their eye on the guy, a checkered shirt on horseback to ride.
When Ferguson charged, through lines he tried, but he was shot from the horse that way.
At Liberties call, his horse did fall into Cleveland's hands that day.

On a pale moon night, spy the white horse light, see
the ghost of bug-a-boo creek.
Ferguson's checkered shirt, and his sword held high,
He rides again to seek.
When Ferguson charged, he did fall and his horse did
get away.
At Liberties call, his horse did fall into Cleveland's
hands that day.
Col. Ben brought him back to his Rhonda farm,
where the white horse ghost still plays.

Cleveland's Revenge

Colonel Benjamin Cleveland was known to be brutal and confrontational when dealing with those loyal to King George III. Records and various accounts indicate that Cleveland executed many Tories during the five or so years that he was active in the Revolutionary cause. Some of those accounts contain bizarre turns and twists that are yet legendary. Cleveland was an animated character of the early American frontier. Large, robust and brutal in war, and quick to hang a Tory, Cleveland was also eager to serve justice in a community affair. Although he is most remembered for his leadership at the Battle of Kings Mountain, this section deals with his bizarre tendency to conduct hangings that have become the stuff of legends.

Accounts of Benjamin Cleveland's hangings go back as far as 1776, when he hanged Tories on the return travel to Wilkes County following the Battle of Moore's Creek Bridge. The Moravians were astonished at the manner of Cleveland's men, who were spotted riding through the Moravian towns (near present day Winston-Salem). They reported that the Wilkes County men appeared as rough frontiersmen, wearing Scottish tartans, kilts and other related clothing. These garments had been looted from the dead bodies of Loyalist Highland Scots at the Moore's Creek Battlefield (north of present-day Wilmington). Cleveland was a man who would establish a brutal reputation during the Southern Campaign of the American Revolution.

Biggerstaff Hangings

During the retreat of the Patriot militia following the Patriot victory on October 7, 1780, at the Battle of Kings Mountain, the Patriot leaders held a trial at Biggerstaff's farm on October 14, 1780. This court was held in the forest located just north of present-day Rutherfordton, North Carolina, and was held to decide the fate of several of the Loyalists accused of hideous acts against the rebel cause. Over six hundred Loyalist prisoners were captured by the victorious Patriots. The Tory prisoners were marched back on the same route that had been the route of pursuit just a few days before. The Patriots decided to hold court for the purpose of convicting the most corrupt Tories for various war crimes against the Patriots, including robbery, house burning and murder.

Based on old journals and accounts, Cleveland was considered by many historians to be the ringleader of the Biggerstaff hangings. Ben Cleveland apparently had a prominent part in the decision-making process. The glare of hundreds of pine knot torches and animated faces circled the convicted war criminals. Under eerie torch light, nine Tories were hanged that night. If the leadership had not called off the grisly affair, most historians agree that up to thirty-two British Tories would have dangled from the trees in the darkened woods. One can say that the reputation of Colonel Cleveland was firmly cemented among those living at the time. Benjamin Cleveland may have the distinguishing record of hanging more men in an American war on American soil than any other person in history.

The area of downtown Wilkesboro near the present Wilkes Heritage Museum saw many episodes that related to the history surrounding the Kings Mountain Campaign. In fact, following the Battle of Kings Mountain, the Tory prisoners were marched by this area of downtown Wilkesboro prior to taking a route that led them through the Moravian towns near present-day Winston-Salem. The sites where Cleveland carried out the hangings have long created mystique and rumors of haunts. One can certainly say that the area of the old buildings in downtown Wilkesboro had a violent past that included capital punishment and public execution.

Could it be that the ghost stories that follow in the coming chapters somehow relate to this violent past?

The Southern Campaign by its nature tended to pit Americans against Americans. The Loyalists, or Tories, were Americans who remained loyal to the king, while the Patriots, or Whigs, were Americans who rebelled against the British Crown. In the South, this trend generally played out to a brutal conflict in which neighbor fought against neighbor and brother against brother. For that turbulent two-year period (1780–81), many were caught up in a very bitter and horrible civil conflict, resulting in a seemingly endless array of mini-wars fought throughout the Carolina backcountry.

THE HANGINGS AT THE TORY OAK

> *Captain Riddle, It is useless to waste your whisky on such efforts.*
>
> —Kings Mountain and Its Heroes, *Lyman C. Draper*

A massive northern black oak stood in Wilkesboro for many years as a symbol of the American struggle for freedom. The Tory Oak was gradually weakened by storms, including Hurricane Hugo in 1989, and several other powerful thunderstorms over the next few years. Then, during a strong, windy storm in 1992, the mighty Tory Oak fell. For over two hundred years, the massive tree had been pointed out to strangers in Town. We'll now take a look at its vivid history.

Brown and Cowles, 1779

During the fall of 1779, two men were apprehended and brought to the meetinghouse in Wilkesboro for robbing a Lincoln County Patriot, Major George Wilfong. The culprits evidently stole everything that they could carry away on horseback. The two noted Tories, Brown (or Jones) and Cowles, even stole Major Wilfong's clothesline in order to use it for halters. Brown and Cowles were hanged with Wilfong's clotheslines on the Tory Oak. Most local

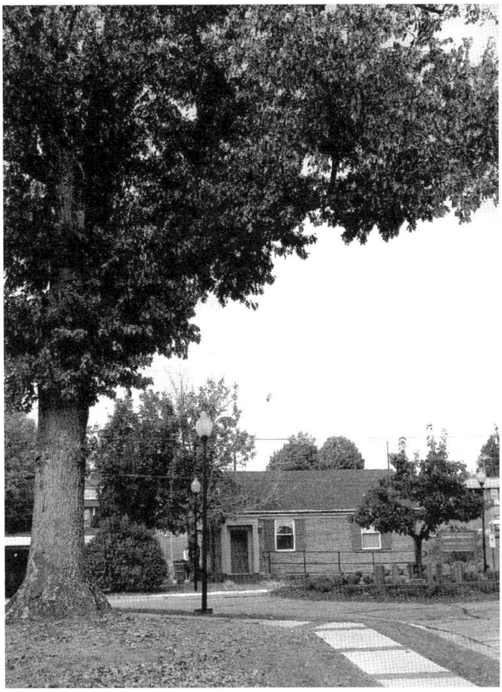

Tory Oak site with Tory Oak Jr. in the foreground. At least five Tories were hanged at this site in the Revolutionary War under Benjamin Cleveland. *Courtesy of the Wilkes Heritage Museum.*

residents considered the hangings just. General Cleveland was later exonerated from a murder charge by the North Carolina General Assembly for his role in the hangings of Brown and Cowles, although the act was labeled by some as summary justice. Although not a lot of details are available, apparently some felt that a fairly swift sentence was given without all the facts presented.

Riddle, Reeves and Goss, Spring of 1781

Following his service at the Battle of Kings Mountain on October 7, 1780, in April 1781, Cleveland was captured by a Tory band at his plantation along the New River near present-day Todd in Ashe County. During the Tory ambush, Cleveland was held at gunpoint by Zachariah Wells. Wells delivered Cleveland to the Tory leaders. Word soon reached Wilkes County that Ben Cleveland had been apprehended and would most likely be taken to British authorities at Ninety Six, South Carolina, for the purpose of execution. No doubt a handsome bounty was awaiting the person or persons who could catch old Colonel Ben. Cleveland would be a prize among the Loyalist partisans.

Fortunately, a Wilkes County posse was dispatched to rescue old roundabout from his confinement. Ben's brother, Captain Robert "Bob" Cleveland, headed out with a rescue party. Horses were readied and the men gave chase. The Tory band was discovered at Riddles Knob in Watauga County. The posse was successful in ambushing the Tories, capturing their leaders and rescuing their famed leader. Colonel Ben Cleveland, upon seeing brother Bob and the Wilkes County boys arrive on the scene, yelled, "Huzzah for Brother Bob—Give them hell boys!"

The captured Tories included their leader, Captain Riddle, and associates Reeves and Goss. They were apprehended, brought to Wilkesboro and hanged on the Tory Oak. Ben found out that Captain Riddle had given whiskey to the guards in order to try and escape. After learning of the plot, Colonel Ben ordered the three hanged promptly after breakfast.

Drapers writes in *Kings Mountain and Its Heroes*:

> *The three notorious freebooters were accordingly executed, on the hill adjoining the village, on a stately oak, which is yet standing, and pointed out to strangers at Wilkesboro. Mrs. Riddle, who seems to have accompanied her husband on his wild and reckless marauds, was present, and witnessed the execution.*

Zachariah Wells

> *Jimmy my son, this a bad man and we must hang all such dangerous Tories to get them out of their misery.*
>
> —Kings Mountain and Its Heroes, *Lyman C. Draper*

Soon after the execution of Riddle, Reeves and Goss at the Tory Oak, Zachariah Wells, the Tory who had held Benjamin Cleveland at gunpoint during the capture at the Old Fields in Ashe County, was caught and brought to Colonel Cleveland. Wells had a reputation for being cunning and brutal. He was considered a dangerous foe and Cleveland seemed pleased at his capture. Wells was conveyed to Hughes Bottom, which was situated along the Yadkin River on the south side of Cleveland's Roundabout Plantation.

At this spot, Zachariah Wells stood beneath a giant sycamore that dangled its limbs over the water. Wells was also in the presence of two young boys, described as a young boy by the name of James Gwyn and his friend, a young black American boy, both of whom were approximately fourteen years old. Accounts indicate that the two young boys felt sorry for the desperate and pitiful subject, who was suffering from an injury that he had obtained during the scuffle with Cleveland. For a few moments, the boys pleaded a case to Colonel Ben to spare the life of Wells. Cleveland replied, "Now my sons, he is a bad man and we must hang all dangerous Tories, and get them out of their misery!" Wells made the following bizarre statement: "Colonel Cleveland, if you hang me here below this spot, no grass will ever grow here again." In the end, Zachariah proved to be right. Indeed no blade of grass grows below that spot because Zachariah eventually swung on a limb extending out over the waters of the Yadkin.

A few years ago, historian Annie Winkler led me down to the site along Hughes Bottom, the present-day site of the Chatham farm, and pointed out to me the mighty sycamore where Zachariah Wells

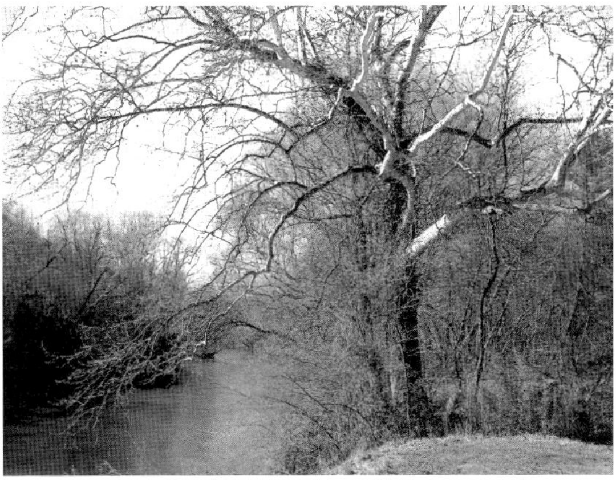

Tory Zachariah Wells was hanged on a giant sycamore by Colonel Benjamin Cleveland in 1781.

was hanged back in 1781. This tree is possibly one of the very last trees in America still standing in which a British soldier was executed during the American Revolution.

The Last Hanging in Wilkes

Some say that Ben Cleveland's ghost stayed around and played havoc at other events, including hangings, for a number of years. In fact, in 1888, at the hanging of James Byers, the last hanging in Wilkes, strange things happened. James Byers shot a man from Allegheny County, apparently over a horse-thieving dispute. Although making a good case for self-defense, James Byers was found guilty of murder. The sentence was that James Byers would hang by the neck until dead, a common sentence of the time.

On the day of the hanging, James Byers was taken to Cub Creek to be baptized. He then met privately with a preacher on the steps of the old law office, which is now known as the Finley Law Office. Deputies then pushed back the crowd and led Mr. Byers in the direction of the gallows. The huge timbers of the gallows were erected behind the Old Wilkes Jail and made an ominous form against the backdrop of the sleepy cornfields along the adjacent river bottom.

People were positioned in all kinds of high perches to get a better view of the gallows. Accounts from old newspaper articles indicate that as many as eight thousand people crowded into town to witness the hanging. People climbed trees and gazed from vantage points such as front porches and the tops of barns and houses.

The rope was attached to Byers's neck and the deputy stepped from the figure of Byers, who stood standing quietly awaiting the inevitable. Then, at the exact time that the command was given, the trapdoor swung open and James Byers fell a few feet to a presumably quick death. But something went terribly wrong and the fall apparently did not break Byers's neck. He struggled in plain view of the crowd. The crowd became very nervous and shocked at the grisly display of human suffering. Accounts indicate that a "mob-like" scene followed as the mass of people broke into a state of pandemonium. Witnesses said that women beat on one another's backs and even tore their own hair out. Men got into fistfights and some fell from trees, injuring themselves. People pushed and shoved and shouted in anger. Bystanders, who were appalled at the situation, pleaded desperately for Byers to be cut down. After a few minutes of wild confusion, the deputies finally regained order. About that time, Byers stopped moving and was soon pronounced dead.

Although the crowd was disbanded and went peacefully along, folks said that this was indeed a bizarre scene. It was believed by some that the old ghost of Colonel Ben Cleveland came back to haunt the last hanging in Wilkes.

The Robert Cleveland House

Today the Robert Cleveland House stands behind the Old Wilkes Jail in downtown Wilkesboro. Built in 1779, the house stood in the Purlear community for over two hundred years. In the mid-1980s, the log home was relocated by a historic preservation carried out by Old Wilkes Inc. Today, Old Wilkes Inc. is Wilkes Heritage Museum and contains four buildings, which include the Old Wilkes County Courthouse (Wilkes Heritage Museum), the Old Wilkes Jail, the Finley Law Office and the Robert Cleveland House.

Robert Cleveland moved from Virginia to what is now Wilkes County about 1775. He settled near the Yadkin River on a tract of land that had been granted to him. During the American Revolutionary War, Robert, along with his brother, Colonel Benjamin Cleveland, took an active part in reprisals against Tories who were often accused of various crimes.

Robert served as captain of a company in his brother's regiment in the Battle of Kings Mountain. This victory of the colonial militia was a significant one in that it forced General Cornwallis to withdraw to South Carolina. After serving his country well throughout the Revolutionary War and in local government and community affairs, Robert died in 1812 at the age of sixty-eight.

Robert "Bob" also rescued his brother Benjamin from a band of Tories during the capture near Todd along the New River in spring of 1781. Bob was a lot like his brother Benjamin. He was a big man physically. He was also an effective leader. Bob's militia apparently anchored the western Wilkes County Patriots. He frequently mustered his forces at nearby Rendezvous Mountain. Robert Cleveland lived in Parsonsville, near the Lewis Fork Creek. The community is now the present-day post office community of Purlear. Bob's brother Ben lived at his Roundabout Plantation, which was near present-day Ronda; at the time, this distance was nearly a day's ride by horseback.

In 1779, the community was on the edge of the hostile frontier and was subject to attacks from wild bears, cougars and hostile Indian tribes who often passed through the area. During the very inflammatory period of the Southern Campaign of the American Revolution, neighbor often fought against neighbor. Today, when touring the Robert Cleveland House, one will notice the old-fashioned wooden drop bars that served to lock the doors from intruders.

During the later part of the twentieth century, the house stood vacant and in a slowly decaying state for a number of years. In 1987, on a project undertaken by Old Wilkes Inc., the log house was disassembled and brought to downtown Wilkesboro for the reassembling and restoration process. The original logs and creek rocks were used to reconstruct the logs, chimneys and fireplaces. The house was restored in close detail, even down to the wooden pegs used to hold together rafters. The Robert Cleveland House is believed to be the oldest house in Wilkes County.

The Cleveland family was big by today's standards but not uncommon at the time. Between fourteen and seventeen people, including Mr. and Mrs. Robert Cleveland, may have lived in the log home at the same time. In fact, the census of 1790 shows the Cleveland household having twenty-four persons, including ten slaves. It is known that Cleveland's farm also produced whiskey, a fact that later appeared in Bob Cleveland's will.

Bob Cleveland had thirteen children by his first wife, Aley Mathis. Aley and one of two twins passed away just a few days before Christmas, on December 18, 1791, about two weeks after the twins were born. A few years later, Robert married Sallie Johnson and produced four children by that marriage

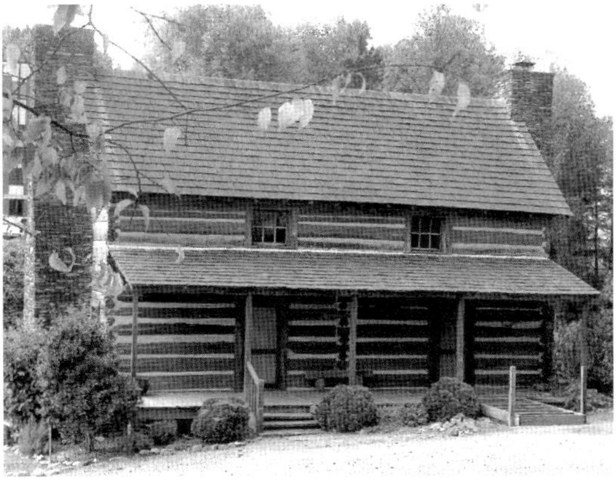

The Robert Cleveland House. *Courtesy of the Wilkes Heritage Museum.*

What is particularly interesting about the Robert Cleveland House is that tour participants sometimes report a woman dressed in colonial clothing rocking by the hearth in the downstairs portion of the two-story structure. Others have noted that the apparition seems to rock through the existing rocker, passing though the stationary rocker in a ghostly vapor.

Could this repeating apparition be one of Robert Cleveland's wives? By the description witnessed, this appears to be the case. Perhaps Mrs. Cleveland is knitting for her children by the comfort of the fireplace, a common scene in the eighteenth century. The odd thing is that several people have reported the same sighting. One volunteer who was in the house in May 2006 mentioned that she felt the presence of an elderly woman in a rocking chair. She experienced this encounter when the lights strangely flickered at a rapid rate. One tour group of schoolchildren asked, "Who is the authentic-looking docent in the rocking chair? She seems too serious. She doesn't seem to respond to our questions!"

Immediately behind the Robert Cleveland House in downtown Wilkesboro is the trail head for the Overmountain Victory Trail and Yadkin River Greenway. One can access this section for a nice hike along the old bottom land by the river. On October 7, 1980 (the 200th anniversary of the Battle of Kings Mountain), the Overmountain Victory National Historic Trail was signed by President Jimmy Carter from a bill introduced by former U.S.

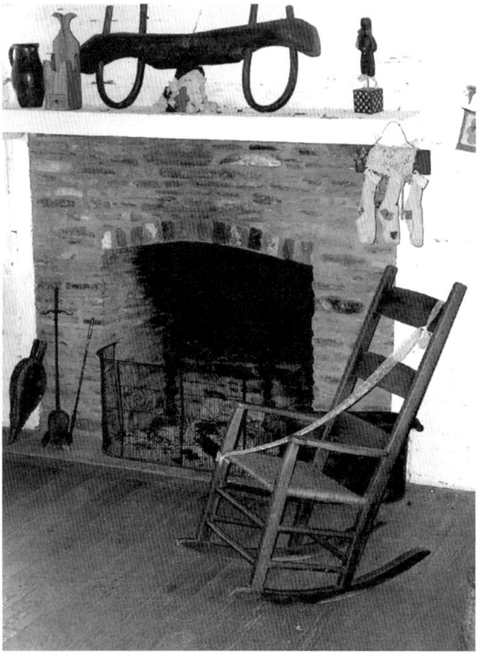

The rocking chair by the hearth in the Robert Cleveland House. *Courtesy of the Wilkes Heritage Museum.*

senator (then U.S. congressman) Jim Broyhill. One can visit sections of this National Historic Trail today and learn about the compelling story of the Battle of Kings Mountain. Wilkesboro and the Wilkes Heritage Museum serve as one of the corridor trail heads of the Overmountain Victory Trail.

WILLIAM LENOIR

William Lenoir (1751–1839), like Robert Cleveland, was a captain in the company under Benjamin Cleveland at the Battle of Kings Mountain. He was a prominent North Carolina statesman in the late eighteenth and early nineteenth century. The city of Lenoir, North Carolina, is named after him. William Lenoir laid out the town of Wilkesboro in the year 1800.

Lenoir was of French Huguenot ancestry and was born in Brunswick County, Virginia. At the age of nine, Lenoir moved with his family to eastern North Carolina. Despite having no formal education, he could read and write Latin, Greek and French. His first occupation was that of teacher and schoolmaster, and he later became a surveyor. While surveying in Western North Carolina, Lenoir decided to permanently settle there. He brought with him his wife, Ann Ballard, and a baby daughter, when he arrived in Wilkes County in March 1775. The Lenoirs had a total of nine children.

Fort Defiance

Early in the movement for independence, Lenoir became an ardent supporter of the American Revolution. Accounts of his bravery during the Battle of Kings Mountain were well documented. Lenoir had his clothing torn from round balls in several places and had a patch of hair shot off the back of his head.

After the war, William and Ann built their home, called Fort Defiance, which is located along today's NC Highway 268 just a few miles east of Lenoir in the Happy Valley Community. Fort Defiance continues today, restored as a tourist and historical attraction. Several reenactments and historic programs are offered there annually, including both Revolutionary War and Civil War reenactments.

Lenoir was a thinker and innovator. Some have compared him to Thomas Jefferson because of his ability to create, plan and design, and because of his understanding of political systems. William Lenoir was a founding member, and the first president, of the board of trustees of the University of North Carolina. Lenoir also served as a member of the state legislature and speaker of the North Carolina Senate. Lenoir passed away on May 6, 1839, at the age of eighty-one years. Today, one can still see the works of Lenoir in downtown Wilkesboro, as the city streets still follow the same layout as when they were designed in 1800. Many also believe that the large sugar berry trees that yet thrive as of this writing in the lawn of the Brown-Cowles House in Wilkesboro were planted by Lenoir himself.

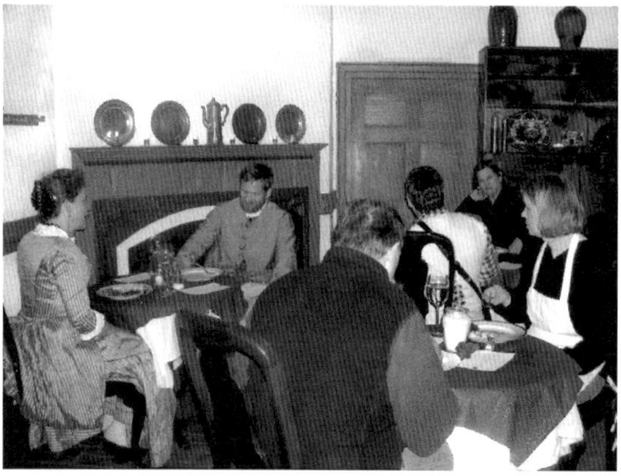

Modern-day folks enjoy a Valentine's Day banquet at Fort Defiance, the former home of William Lenoir. *Photo by Heather Osborne.*

THE HAUNTS OF FORT DEFIANCE

Fort Defiance is a marvelously well-preserved historic site. It contains more original artifacts than Mount Vernon or Monticello. With all its history, Fort Defiance also has reported hauntings.

Historian and docent Jeff Neale told of a recent ghost sighting that he experienced at Fort Defiance during December 2008. One night as the staff was wrapping up the Candlelight Ghost Tours through the Lenoir home, he caught a glimpse of something running down the steps and into a room on the first floor. He described an apparition that appeared as a young boy wearing knee britches and a blue eighteenth-century waistcoat. The period of the clothing would have been a good fit for one of Lenoir's sons. It would have been perfectly normal to see the youngster running down the steps to play in the yard of this fine colonial home. Lenoir's descendants continued to live and raise their families at the fort for many years. In the late 1870s, Sarah Gwyn Lenoir saw an apparition of a mulatto child playing in the box shrub garden next to the house. Historical records later confirmed that a child fitting the description of the sighting previously lived near the Lenoir home during the nineteenth century.

CHAPTER 5

GHOSTS OF THE NINETEENTH CENTURY

THE BROWN—COWLES HOUSE

During a particularly memorable ghost tour during the summer of 2008, the group stood in an approximately eighteen- by twenty-foot plank building known as the slave quarters that stands behind the historic Brown-Cowles House in downtown Wilkesboro. Members of the Winston-Salem Paranormal Society as well as participants of the tour that night captured orbs (small circles of light that appear in photographs) while in the old slave quarters. Many in the group also noted the presence of cold spots. All those present talked about a strange feeling of presence during the evening. Since that night, the visit to the slave quarters has become a popular stop on the Candlelight Ghost Tours in downtown Wilkesboro.

The small building is one of the few examples of slave quarters still standing in America. It is known that a former owner of the estate, Hamilton Brown, built the central core of the house shortly after 1834. It was considered the finest home in Wilkesboro for many years. In addition to the slave quarters, a slave kitchen and curing house still stand nearby. These buildings were occupied and used by black American slaves prior to the War Between the States. Brown owned as many as fourteen slaves who at times occupied the slave quarters.

The original portion of the house was a two-story frame structure. A porch ran across the front. A two-story wing, generally believed

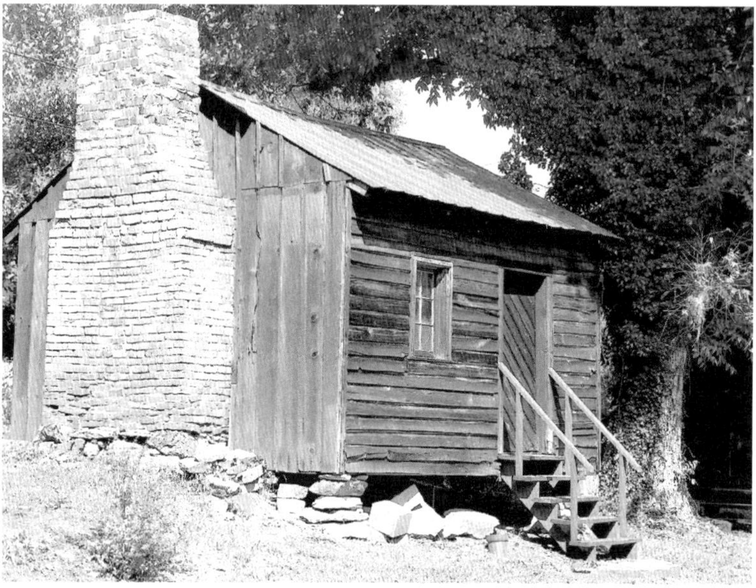

Old slave quarters behind the Brown-Cowles House.

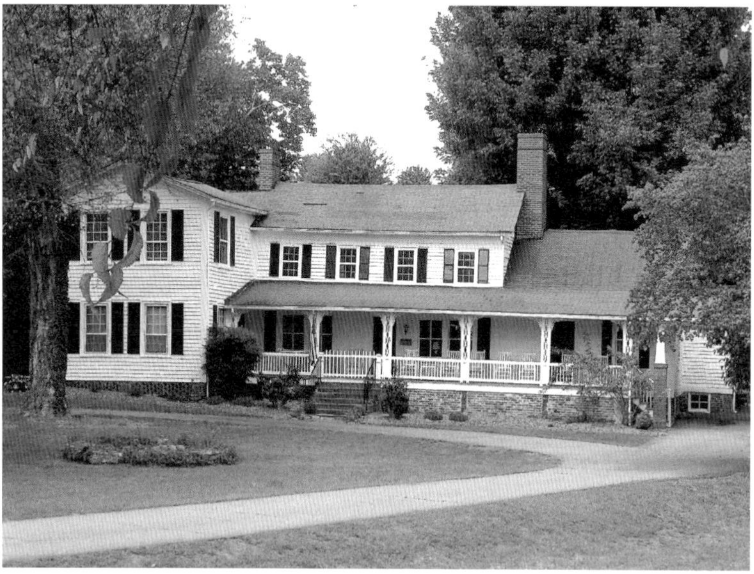

The Brown-Cowles House in downtown Wilkesboro.

to have been built by W.H.H. Cowles, was added to the southwest corner of the house sometime before 1871. A one-story addition on the east side of the house was likely built around 1896 and the final additions were added sometime between 1920 and 1926.

William Henry Harrison Cowles

William H.H. Cowles (1840–1901) was a politician who served four terms in the United States House of Representatives. Originally a native of Yadkin County, Cowles served in General Lee's Army of Northern Virginia and was a member of the Ninth Regiment of the First North Carolina Cavalry. He enlisted on May 16, 1861, and was eventually promoted to lieutenant colonel by the war's end. He fought under J.E.B. Stuart and led Stuart's rear guard during Stuart's "ride around McClellan." Cowles was wounded twice during the war and was considered a war hero by many Wilkes County citizens.

After the war, he practiced law in Wilkesboro. In 1884, he was elected as a Democrat to the Forty-ninth United States Congress. While in Congress, Cowles chaired the Committee on Expenditures in the Department of Justice (Fiftieth Congress) and the Committee on Mines and Mining (Fifty-second Congress). He did not run for reelection in 1892. William H.H. Cowles is buried in the Wilkesboro Town Cemetery.

The current owners are Marilyn and Eric Payne, who inherited the house from Paul Osborne, a prominent citizen and former pioneer of the timber industry in Wilkes County. Marilyn Payne, a board member with Wilkes Heritage Museum, has done vast amounts of research on the development of the interpretive exhibits in the Heritage Museum. Her husband, Eric, is one of the original Candlelight Ghost Tour guides in downtown Wilkesboro.

Stoneman's Raid

During late March 1865, the Civil War was winding down. However, the impact of four years of fighting was being made known in

Western North Carolina, where things were coming to a boil. U.S. General George Stoneman and over six thousand Union troops were marching from the direction of Boone, North Carolina, into the Yadkin Valley. With orders to destroy but not to fight battles, the effect on the area mountain people was completely demoralizing.

General Stoneman was powerfully built, standing at six feet, four inches, and having a face that bore the fruits of a long, hard-fought war. Stoneman's convoy was impressive, with artillery pieces, supply wagons, ambulances and mule teams, and was heavily armed with seasoned able horsemen.

On March 29, 1865, General Stoneman's forces entered Wilkesboro. Tensions were high among the area residents, who had learned that several area towns had been hit hard by Stoneman. Stoneman encountered Confederate resistance in Boone, which resulted in sixty-eight captured and nine killed Confederates. In addition, the town's jail was burned to the ground. Looting and pillaging occurred throughout the countryside and Wilkesboro seemed to be the next target for destruction. In Wilkes, Stoneman left a trail of violence, home robberies and farm pillaging. Those incidents resulted in bushwhacking tales that remain legends today.

Soon after Stoneman rode into town, tradition says that a meeting was held near the intersection of the Cowles driveway and Main Street in downtown Wilkesboro. This meeting supposedly took place between Calvin J. Cowles, who was the half brother of H.H. Cowles, and General Stoneman. Calvin J. Cowles, a Unionist, may have been on better terms and perhaps in a better position than anyone else in Wilkesboro to negotiate with the Union general. The story is that both men were Masons. Whether such a meeting ever took place, General Stoneman chose not to burn Wilkesboro.

Following encampment in the bottomland along the river, Stoneman and his army left the area headed for Dobson and Mount Airy. Although Wilkesboro was spared, Stoneman's raid did have a demoralizing effect on the citizens. While the Federal troops were in the area, they searched homes of known Confederate soldiers for valuables and looted nearby farms for food and supplies. Union soldiers seized the former horse of local CSA General James B. Gordon, who had fought under J.E.B. Stuart and had been killed at

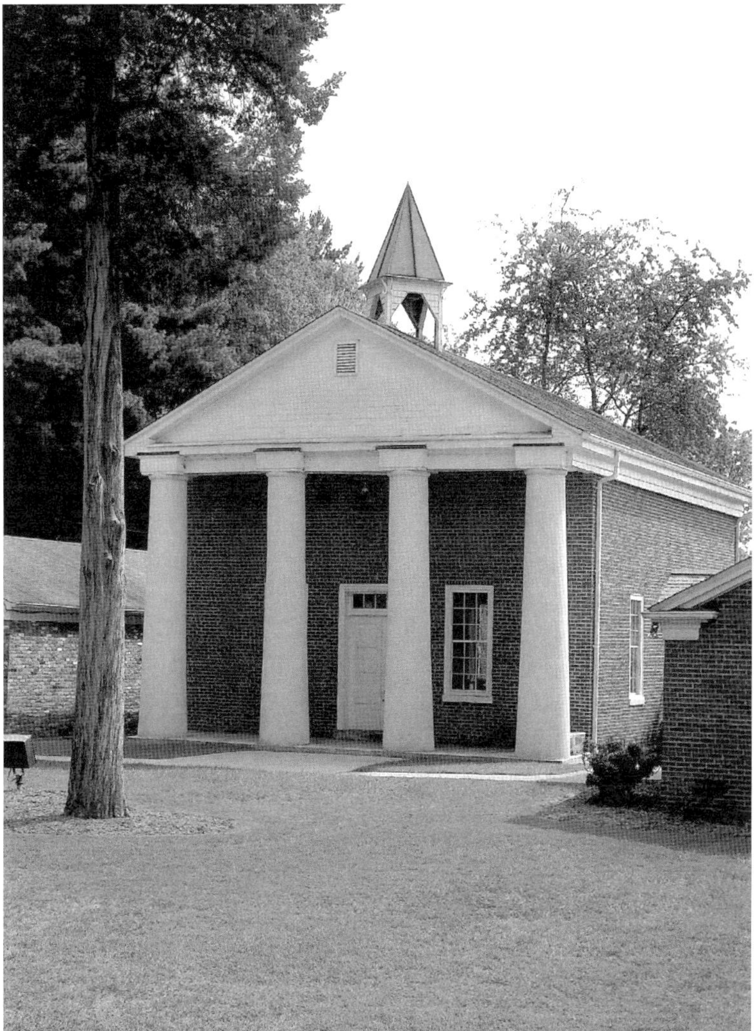

The Wilkesboro Presbyterian Chapel in downtown Wilkesboro was standing during Stoneman's raid.

Spotsylvania about a year earlier. The captured horse was paraded in a humiliating fashion in plain view of General Gordon's family at his former home, Oakland.

VANISHING LADY ON HORSEBACK

A common story that people have passed down from Stoneman's raid is that when General Stoneman's men would send out their advance guards or scouts to check for possible Confederate resistance, the Union scouts would strangely disappear.

A Confederate soldier was killed by Union bushwhackers for concealing the location of Home Guard men. The Union bushwhacker apparently shot the Home Guard man in his own yard while his dear wife watched the scene. The soldier's widow grieved so much that she fell ill and soon died. As Stoneman's army moved through the area, like other invading armies, the men were attracted to young ladies of the community. Union soldiers out on scouting patrol would reportedly be lured by a beautiful female rider on horseback who invited the Union horsemen to a location for the purpose of an intimate arrangement. As the scouts eagerly followed in pursuit, they would suddenly be killed by Confederate guns waiting in ambush. The ghostly female rider was never captured. It was said that she was the spirit of the dead widow returning to seek revenge for her lost Confederate husband.

TRAGIC BUGGY ACCIDENT AT BROWN—COWLES

Several years after the Civil War, a young woman was riding a buggy through Wilkesboro when the buggy overturned and the woman was thrown and badly injured. Following the accident, she was laid in a shallow depression in the driveway at the Brown-Cowles House in downtown Wilkesboro while a doctor was called to assist. Unfortunately, the woman died, and many local people grieved her loss.

Today during ghost tours, people often note the presence of a cold spot at the location where the young lady lay dying during the terrible accident in the late 1800s. Our ghost guides have frequently had participants on the ghost tours take photos of strange lights or orbs at this location. During a ghost tour in the summer of 2008, a person indicated that he felt a hand touch him on the back of the shoulder at this location. To be sure, this is one of the most active and "chilling" points of the downtown Wilkesboro walking ghost tours. Be sure and bring your camera!

Fort Hamby

The book *Bushwhackers* and the movie *Cold Mountain* brought to light the tremendous struggle that took place in Wilkes and the surrounding counties during the Civil War. One such struggle resulted in a famous post–Civil War battle. This was a struggle that involved murder, robbery and feelings of civil disorder and lawlessness. It was known as the Battle of Fort Hamby and it took place in western Wilkes County along the Yadkin River.

Throughout the Civil War, a place known as Fort Hamby was frequented by young men of both sides, Union and Confederate. It was said to be a house of ill repute. The Hamby farmhouse was on the north side of the Yadkin River at the confluence with Lewis Fork Creek. The site had a commanding 360-degree view of the countryside and was considered to be an excellent place for defending from attack. In fact, a century earlier, Daniel Boone had established a homeplace close by along the Yadkin River. It may be that Boone likewise chose the location for its defensive posture in case of a hostile Indian attack.

During Stoneman's raid of March 1865, a detachment of bushwhackers broke off from General Stoneman's army and deserted. The deserters were divided into two bands, one under Captain Simmons and one under Captain Wade. From this point, Simmons operated an outlaw band in the Brushy Mountains while Captain Wade made his outlaw post at Fort Hamby.

The house that Wade chose and fortified was near the road that led from Wilkesboro to Lenoir and was less than a half mile from Holman's Ford, a popular fording spot on the Yadkin. The house was a two-story log structure and was fortified with many guns, gunpowder and provisions. Wade had his men cut extra ports in the log walls for their guns on the second story of the building. The term "Fort Hamby" related to the intent of Wade and his men to prevent any attackers from succeeding in penetrating their stronghold.

Wade's men wasted no time in terrorizing the countryside. Robberies and attacks on innocent citizens took place. The group conducted plundering raids as far away as Alexander and Caldwell Counties. In one tragic episode, an innocent child was shot for apparent target practice as the youngster was climbing a fence in a field near Holeman's Ford. In yet another report, Wade's men captured a man who secretly hid gold from Union forces during Stoneman's raid. The outlaw band tied the man to a tree and began skinning him with their Bowie knives until he told them where his gold was hidden.

In May 1865, area residents had had enough of Wade's raiders. Attacks were planned and set in motion by ex-Confederate soldiers returning from the war and tired of living in fear. Major Harvey Bingham led the first attack on Fort Hamby to try to capture the bandits. Although he was nearly successful in pulling off the attack, Bingham slipped up when he allowed Wade to catch him off guard with a trick. While Bingham's men were allowing the prisoners time to change clothes, the captives turned the tables and killed two of Bingham's men, after which they were able to escape.

The second attack was mounted a few days later when twenty-two men, including several former Confederate officers, opened fire on Fort Hamby. The volume and precision of the returned shots forced them to retreat.

After these two failed attempts to take Fort Hamby, Colonel Wallace Sharpe assembled two companies of men from surrounding counties to eliminate Wade and his men. Finally, on May 19, 1865, Colonel Sharp and the large force completely surrounded Wade and his bandit army posted in Fort Hamby. Reports indicated that heavy gunfire continued back and forth all day and into the night. Only after two men set fire to the house did Wade and his men finally ask for the terms of surrender. Wade sent a message to Colonel Sharp: "Come on, I'm looking for you. I can Whip a Thousand of You!"

Sharpe's reply was, "We'll shoot you." Finally, torches were used to fire the building, and many of the bushwhackers came out with their hands up. Wade managed to escape but four of his men were captured, tied to a stake and executed. Inside the house, the victors found a wealth of stolen goods. Once the valuables had been removed, the house was burned to the ground. Wade made a mad dash amid heavy fire toward the river and was never found. A few months later, reports came from the northern states that Wade had breathed through a piece of river cane in a low bushy place along the Yadkin River and then made his escape later when Sharpe's men abandoned the search.

Today, the site of Fort Hamby is a public recreation area managed by the U.S. Army Corps of Engineers at W. Kerr Scott Lake. Recently, the Corps, with the help of community partnerships, built a large outdoor amphitheatre that is only a few hundred feet from the old battle site. At this amphitheatre, the Wilkes Playmakers have performed two plays that focus on powerful legends of the Yadkin Valley. Those two plays—*Tom Dooley, A Wilkes County Legend* and *Moonshine and Thunder*—were written by playwright Karen Wheeling Reynolds. For several seasons, I have been on the cast of the Dooley play. During opening night in 2006, when we reenacted the Battle of Fort Hamby, strange chills ran in my veins.

The story of the Battle of Fort Hamby was repeated in a Walt Disney film called *A Menace on the Mountain*, which aired on the old "Wonderful World of Disney" series and ran on TV several years ago. Since those conflicts took place on the old site called Fort Hamby, local folks have talked about strange things happening in this area.

THE PAINTING OF GENERAL JAMES B. GORDON

Visitors to the Old Wilkes Jail often have noted the painting of Confederate general James B. Gordon on the first floor. Strange experiences have been reported regarding this portrait of the CSA general. On tours, single ladies often say that his painting appears to flirt with or wink at them.

James Byron Gordon was born on November 22, 1822, on a homeplace known as Oakland, which was situated on the north side of the Yadkin River near the confluence with the Reddies River, at the present-day site of Wilkes Regional Medical Center. After Gordon was educated at Emory and Henry College, near Abingdon, Virginia, he returned to Wilkes, engaged in a successful mercantile business and became active in politics. In 1850, he was elected to represent the county in the lower house of the North Carolina General Assembly. His grandfather, Charles Gordon, fought under

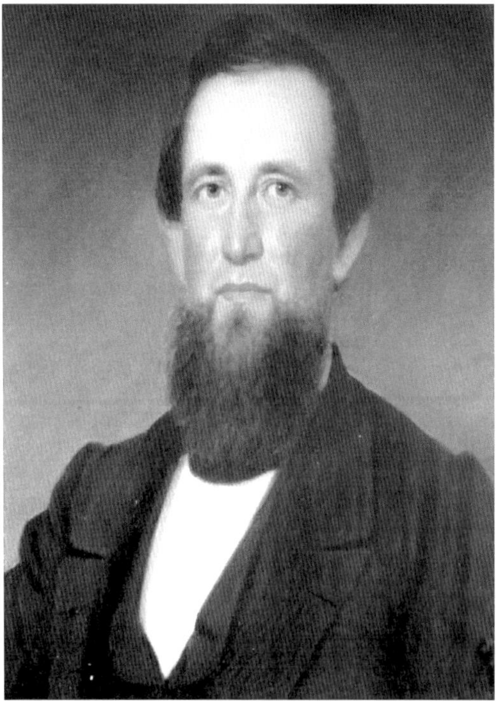

CSA general James B. Gordon's portrait hangs in the Old Wilkes Jail. *Courtesy of the Wilkes Heritage Museum.*

Colonel Benjamin Cleveland in the Battle of Kings Mountain in the Revolutionary War. This pride in his family's military tradition no doubt led to James's leadership in the Confederate army during the Civil War.

At the outbreak of the Civil War, Gordon was one of the first to answer the call, serving in some of the largest and most pivotal battles, including Manassas, Gettysburg, Culpepper, Jack's Shop, Brandy Station, the Wilderness, Spotsylvania, Petersburg and many others. General Gordon rose to the rank of brigadier general and rode under the command of General J.E.B. Stuart. He was a major factor in the success of Stuart's campaigns during the war.

General Gordon was considered to be one of the most eligible bachelors in the entire Confederate army. Even General Stuart took notice of Gordon's ability to gracefully charm fine ladies from Virginia. Gordon was in his age of wisdom, in his thirties, when the war broke out, and he was no doubt considered a great catch among the fine women in the gentry class of the South.

Then in early 1864, General Gordon fell in love with seventeen-year-old Aurelia Halsey of Lynchburg, Virginia, after he met her at a social event near Richmond. "He described her face as beautiful, radiant, even with a smile so bright as to imprint his soul with marks of burning fire." Additional details and correspondence of the romance are described at length in Chris J. Hartley's book *Stuart's Tarheels*.

Thus began an intense and romantic courtship. Though they were passionate and devoted to each other, their courtship did not last long. General Gordon shared with Aurelia a premonition of something dark that he felt was about to occur. A short time later, in May 1864, Gordon was mortally wounded from a bullet on a battlefield just outside of Richmond, Virginia. General Gordon received his mortal wound during the fight at Brook Church on May 12, 1864, and died six days later. His remains were brought home and buried in St. Paul's Episcopal Cemetery at Wilkesboro. His last resting place is marked by a tall monument situated in the beautifully landscaped cemetery.

Today, when young, single ladies come in the Old Wilkes Jail, many glance curiously at the painting of General James B. Gordon.

Young ladies often remark that no matter where they are standing in the room, General Gordon's eyes seem to always be looking directly at them. Some have even become frightened at what they describe as flirting gestures from the portrait hanging on the wall. When young ladies capture a flirting glance from the painting at the Old Wilkes Jail, could it be that General Gordon is still looking for Aurelia?

Dead Man's Hollow

During the troubled times of the Civil War, bushwhacking incidents abounded throughout the Yadkin Valley. The civil conflict became intense partly because Western North Carolina was generally more sympathetic to the Union. Although it's true that Wilkes County supplied a large number of men for the Confederacy, some also fought and served for the Union.

The Confederate Home Guard operated like a militia during the War Between the States. The presence of the Home Guard often exacerbated the intensity of this civil conflict. This "backwoods militia" sometimes attempted to enforce the Confederate draft, creating strife and disapproval among the citizens. In addition, not all of the Home Guard members were upstanding citizens, and some became involved in bloody bushwhacking episodes in the backcountry. Legends, tales and ghost stories still exist about this violent period in history.

My great-great-grandfather, Lewis Absher (1848–1935), was born and raised in the Mulberry community of Wilkes County. When the Civil War broke out, he became interested in fighting for the Confederacy. He was only thirteen years old when the War Between the States began in 1861. Because he was too young to join the army, he joined the Wilkes County Home Guard. Near the time of Stoneman's raid, which took place in March 1865, Absher became heavily involved in various bushwhacking raids. Unfortunately, one of these conflicts took place a few months after Appomattox and thus after the conclusion of the Civil War. What might have been a war incident turned into the crime of murder.

During Stoneman's raid, a local group of Union sympathizers, led by a man named Harrison Tinsley, apparently reported to General Stoneman's men the whereabouts of homes and property belonging to members of the Home Guard. Absher and other Home Guard soldiers barely escaped with their lives. A few months later, after the war was already over, Lewis and his fellow Home Guard members learned of the plot that had been initiated by Tinsley.

Tinsley was rounded up and captured by a search party led by Absher and subsequently brought to a small barn in a hollow along Mulberry Creek. The site is located in a narrow gorge adjacent to present-day NC Highway 18, north of the Mulberry community. Tinsley was then executed in a technique known as "slow hanging." Slow hanging allows the victim to struggle for longer because the feet of the dying victim were just close enough to the floor to occasionally bounce and release the noose just long enough to gasp a breath or two of air, thus prolonging the agony. Because this hanging took place after the Civil War was over, Absher was charged with murder. Lewis Absher wasted no time in fleeing from Wilkes. He left for Tennessee and waited out a length of seven years before returning to Scottsville in adjacent Alleghany County. In 1865, a loophole in the law existed known as the "Statutes of Limitations Clause." One could move out of state for seven years and then return, immune from conviction of a North Carolina crime. Thus, Absher escaped having to go to trial for the murder of Harrison Tinsley.

This incident connects to part of the Tom Dooley story in an account passed down by Lewis Absher's daughter, Mary Etta, my great-grandmother. Apparently, her father Lewis knew Tom Dula ("Tom Dooley") very well; both were from Wilkes and had served for the Confederacy. Following the disappearance of Laura Foster, Tom Dooley heard that Lewis Absher had successfully escaped to Tennessee following the hanging of sympathizer Tinsley. It is told that Tom Dooley then attempted the same thing a few months after Absher's escape. Unfortunately for Dooley, this copycat attempt to run off to Tennessee was not as successful. Tom Dooley was captured along Doe Creek in eastern Tennessee by Colonel James

Grayson and a Wilkes County posse and was brought back to the Wilkes County jail. When I gave this account to Karen Reynolds, she wrote it into her play, *Tom Dooley, a Wilkes County Legend.*

Today in the Mulberry community in Wilkes County there is a site that for over one hundred years has been known as Dead Man's Hollow. People are afraid to go up there at night because of the reports of strange sounds. Some report hearing the moaning sounds of a man who is dying and gasping for breath. Apparently, the cries for help are accompanied by other voices that are taunting and laughing at the sad victim.

The site is along a narrow gorge adjacent to NC Highway 18 North near Bumgarner's Country Store. When I was a youngster in the 1960s, my cousins and I used to play army by the creek when visiting my Uncle John. Little did I know at the time that the site had witnessed a brutal hanging of the Union sympathizer by my great-great-grandfather Lewis Absher. I was totally unaware that Lewis Absher had anything to do with the Tom Dooley story! I was surprised to later learn that because of this grisly history, Dead Man's Hollow is considered to be haunted.

CHAPTER 6

TOM DOOLEY

Today, folks theorize that they can hear Ann Melton's and Tom Dooley's ghosts locked in an eternal struggle in the Old Wilkes Jail. It seems to be an act repeated over and over again on cool, stormy days. For years, a past curator of the Old Wilkes Jail heard noises of feet walking around or climbing the stairs. At times the noise was as if people were in a fight or locked in a perpetual struggle. Recently, the Old Wilkes Jail has been a subject of paranormal investigation teams and is a favorite spot on the Heritage Museum's Candlelight Ghost Tours. The mystery of the infamous love triangle began as a story immediately following the Civil War. When Confederate soldier Thomas C. Dula (Dooley) returned home to Ferguson after the war, he renewed an old relationship with Ann Melton, his former sweetheart.

Ann Foster Melton was married to a shoemaker, James Melton, and this romance between Ann and Tom Dooley became inflamed as rumors circulated in the community. Early in 1866, Tom began courting Ann's first cousin, Laura Foster. Evidently, this is when trouble started to brew. The following spring, Laura and Tom broke off their relationship until one day when Laura told Tom that she was with child. Apparently, Tom and Laura then made plans to run off to Tennessee to be married. Meanwhile, Laura's cousin, Ann, became extremely jealous after learning of the wedding plans between Tom and Laura.

On a warm spring day in late May 1866, Laura Foster rode off on her father's mare in the direction of the Bates Place. Presumably, she was going to meet Tom to run off and get married. However, the outcome proved to be a much different one. Laura was apparently ambushed at the Bates Place in a hidden grove of pines and died of a stab wound in the chest. Search parties did not find her body until late August or early September.

Laura's partially decomposed body was discovered in a shallow grave on a steep hillside about five hundred yards from the presumed murder site. It appeared that following the murder, the body was dragged along a shallow stream in order to mask the ability of search dogs to pick up the scent. Meanwhile, Tom Dooley fled to Tennessee, since he was suspected in the murder of Laura Foster. Another first cousin, Pauline Foster (pronounced "Perline"), had also figured into the complicated affair. Perline, who was staying with Ann and James Melton as a housekeeper, also had intimate relations with Tom Dooley. Perline turned state evidence against Ann Melton and she was arrested and placed in the Old Wilkes Jail.

A Wilkes County posse, with the assistance of retired Union colonel James Grayson of eastern Tennessee, captured Tom while he was washing his feet in a mountain stream near Mountain City, Tennessee. Tom was brought back to Wilkesboro and also placed in the Old Wilkes Jail. For a brief time, Tom and Ann were confined in adjoining cells. Tom was defended by former Confederate North Carolina governor Zebulon Vance. Because of local bias in the matter, Vance convinced the courts to move the trial to Iredell County.

The trial received heightened interest and caught the attention of media both locally and as far away as New York. The old court records showed an emotional exchange from the witnesses called in the case. Considered to be damaging were the testimonies of both Perline Foster and Ann Melton's mother, Lotty Foster. Tom was convicted of murder and later lost an appeal.

On May 1, 1868, almost two years after Laura Foster vanished at the old Bates Place in western Wilkes County, Tom Dooley was hanged for the murder of Laura Foster. Over six thousand people

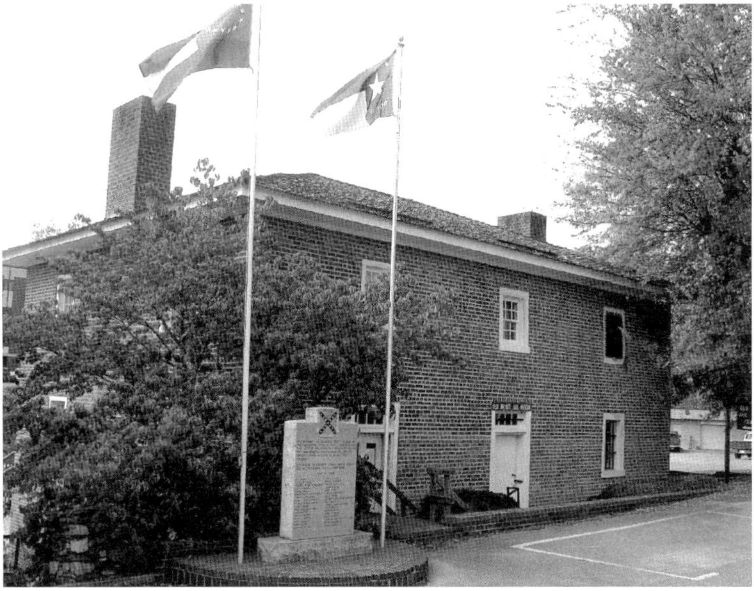

The Old Wilkes Jail was occupied by the infamous Tom Dula/Dooley. *Courtesy of the Wilkes Heritage Museum.*

showed up near the train depot in downtown Statesville, North Carolina. Here are the words to the chorus made popular by the Kingston Trio in a song that was made famous back in 1958 as a national hit song:

Hang down your head Tom Dooley, hang down your head and cry
Hang down your head Tom Dooley, poor boy you're bound to die.

Even more haunting lyrics were found in an older version often sung by Doc Watson:

I dug the grave four feet wide and I dug it four feet deep.
I rolled the cold clay over her and packed it with my feet.
I know they're going to hang me, tomorrow I'll be dead

Though I never harmed a hair on poor little Laura's head.
You can take my old violin and play it if you please
For this time tomorrow boys, it will be of no use to me.

Tom Dooley was listed as a musician in the Confederate army and often delighted the area young ladies by playing the fiddle at local dances. Some have said that perhaps Tom Dooley himself wrote some of the words of the above songs while he was in jail awaiting the inevitable, hanging from a rope for the death of Laura Foster.

Although Ann Melton was acquitted, many were convinced that she had something to do with the murder. According to some, she may have even made a bizarre deathbed confession. World-famous musician Doc Watson heard such accounts from his grandmother, who grew up in the nearby community of Stony Fork and knew the Melton family. Apparently, Ann, who became severely ill just before her death, was tormented by the illusions of burning flesh, of cats climbing her bedpost and of the sounds of frying meat in hell.

A reporter from *Images* magazine toured the Old Wilkes Jail during the summer of 2006. As he was standing just outside the jail cell where Tom Dooley was detained, the reporter asked, "How did they bring Tom Dooley in?" I answered, "In ball and chains." Immediately after I completed that statement, both the reporter and I heard a distinctive sound on the floor. It was like the sound of a large chain and ball (sounding like a log chain) sliding and dropping across the floor as if being propelled by a prisoner! I looked at the reporter and he looked at me. I was almost numb with astonishment. Following the incident, the reporter never again returned.

Other inmates may have also contributed to the haunts of the Old Wilkes Jail. The famous outlaw Otto Wood was also jailed there for stealing a bicycle at age thirteen. The Old Wilkes Jail is one of the few jails from which Wood did not escape. And in its long history, many others have been jailed there for a variety of crimes, including larceny, failure to pay alimony, disorderly conduct and murder. I'm sure that if they could talk, these gray cell walls would tell many tales.

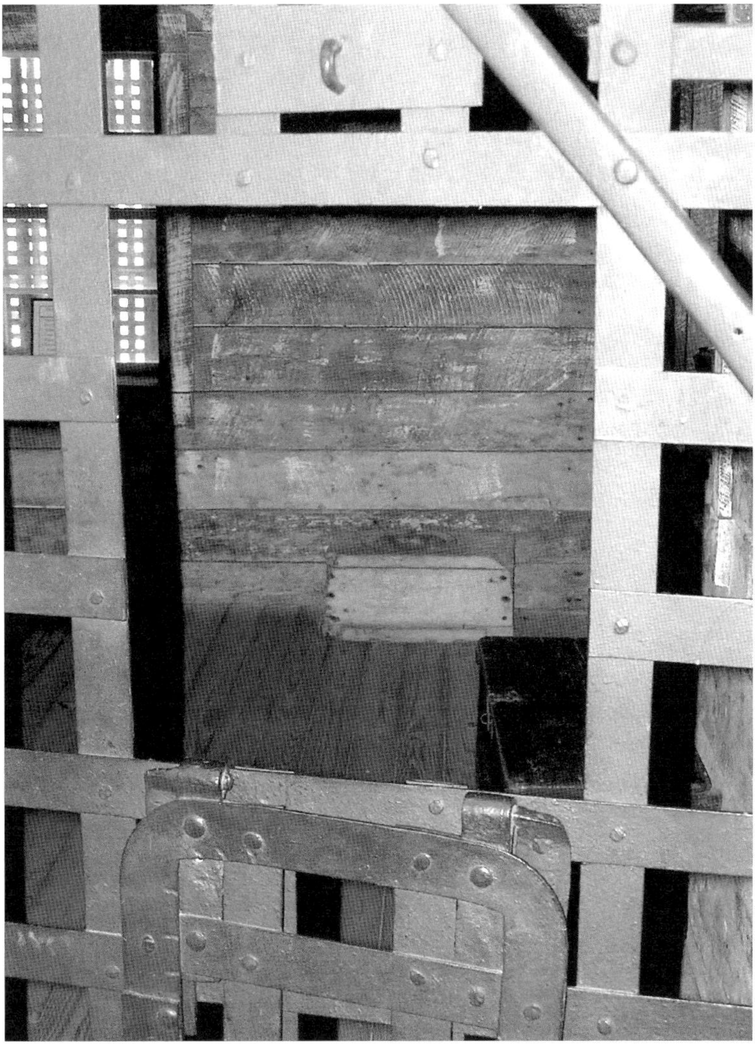

The Old Wilkes Jail. *Courtesy of the Wilkes Heritage Museum.*

During a paranormal investigation conducted in 2007 by the Eastern Paranormal Community, several electronic voice phenomena (EVP) sounds were recorded in the Old Wilkes Jail.

Among the recordings included the sounds of heavy labored breathing, animal groans and the odd sounds of a woman's voice. The female voice sounded as if it were in a Native American language. Could it be that the Old Wilkes Jail stands over an ancient Indian burial site? Or could it be that the past inmates of the Old Wilkes Jail still are trying to speak out, or perhaps live out, their experience of being locked up? Could it be that Tom Dooley and Ann Melton are locked in an eternal struggle or argument over the death of Laura Foster? Today, the Old Wilkes Jail is open for folks to visit and to search out these answers for themselves.

AUTHOR'S NOTE: The outdoor drama *Tom Dooley, a Wilkes County Legend*, which runs annually during summers at Fort Hamby Park at W. Kerr Scott Reservoir, is highly recommended. The play was written by Karen Reynolds and is a very powerful and compelling production.

WHIPPOORWILL ACADEMY

Nestled along NC 268 near the Yadkin River in the rolling countryside of Ferguson, North Carolina, is an interesting heritage site known as Whippoorwill Academy. Each year, many tourists and history buffs visit the site to see the replica Daniel Boone Cabin and artifacts related to the story of Tom Dooley.

One of the major features of Whippoorwill Academy is the one-room schoolhouse built in 1880 by Andy Gould, a well-known carpenter and miller. In addition, Whippoorwill also contains a replica Daniel Boone Cabin, a country store, a blacksmith shop, a jail, a chapel and a reconstructed tavern. The owner, Edith Marie Carter, is an artist, folklorist and historian. The site was once the location of the school of James Larkin Pearson, who served as North Carolina's poet laureate.

Highlights for those who visit Whippoorwill are artifacts such as a lock of Laura Foster's hair and paintings that depict aspects and details about the story of Tom Dula/Dooley.

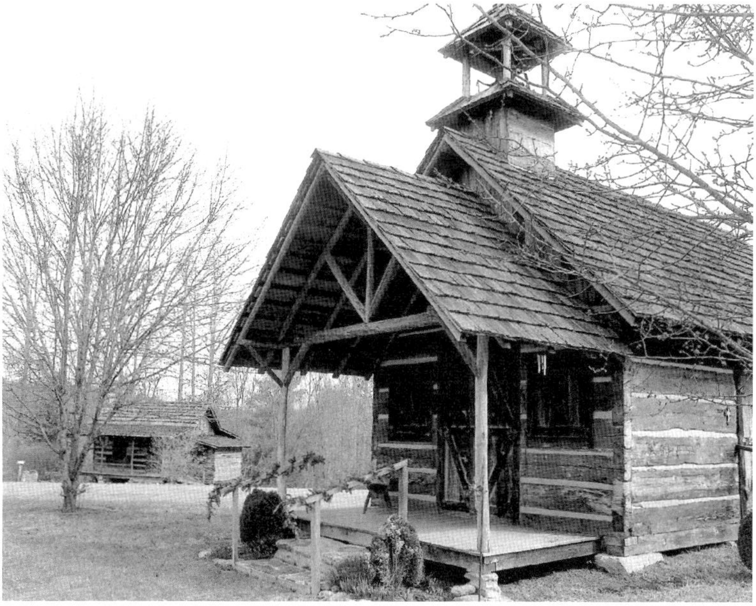

Whippoorwill Academy contains interpretive exhibits and old buildings depicting life along the Yadkin Valley in earlier times.

Tom Dooley Road

Just a short distance from Whippoorwill Academy is Tom (Dula) Dooley Road. A roadside marker indicates Dooley's gravesite. After Tom was hanged in Statesville on May 1, 1868, his body was brought to his home overlooking the Yadkin River. The body was laid on his old featherbed during the wake and blood soaked onto the floor below the bed, creating a stain that was visible for many years.

Later, when Tom's mother and sisters moved away, renters lived in the house and everyone in the family had to sleep in Tom's room because of the bloodstains. People reported hearing moaning, groaning and the clanking of chains. Accounts included seeing white objects or mists float in and out of the doors and windows.

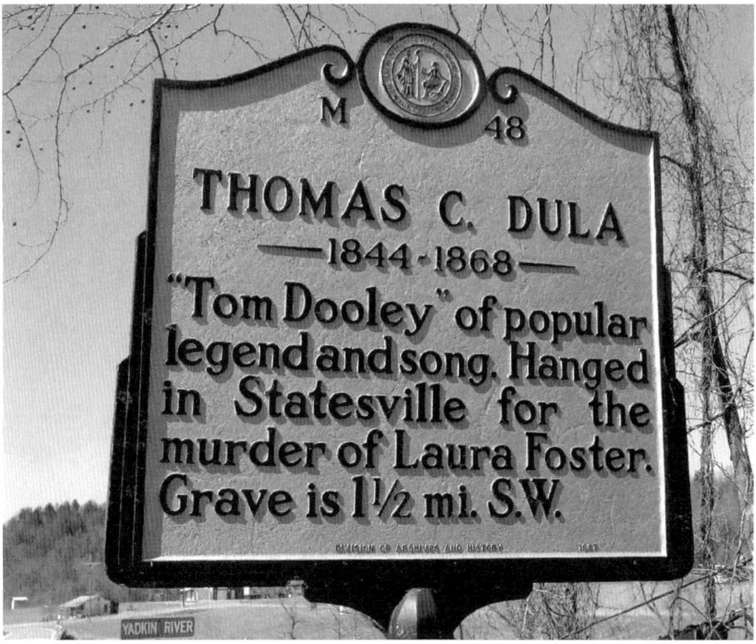

The Tom Dula/Dooley roadside marker in Ferguson along NC Highway 268.

NELLIE

Tom was buried on a hill near a sharp curve on Tom (Dula) Dooley Road. There was a family who lived nearby and had a beautiful daughter named Nellie. Her parents allowed Nellie to attend a party in a one-room schoolhouse nearby. She had fun dancing and playing games with her friends. It was getting late and it was time for the party to end. Since it was late, some of the young men, who delighted in befriending Nellie, suggested that they accompany her home. Nellie refused and rode off into the night on horseback. As she entered the steep curve in the road at Tom Dooley's grave, the horse became spooked and reared, throwing Nellie to the ground. A short time after, her friends came along the way to see a riderless horse near Nellie's lifeless body lying on the roadside. Nellie died just a few feet away from Tom Dooley's grave.

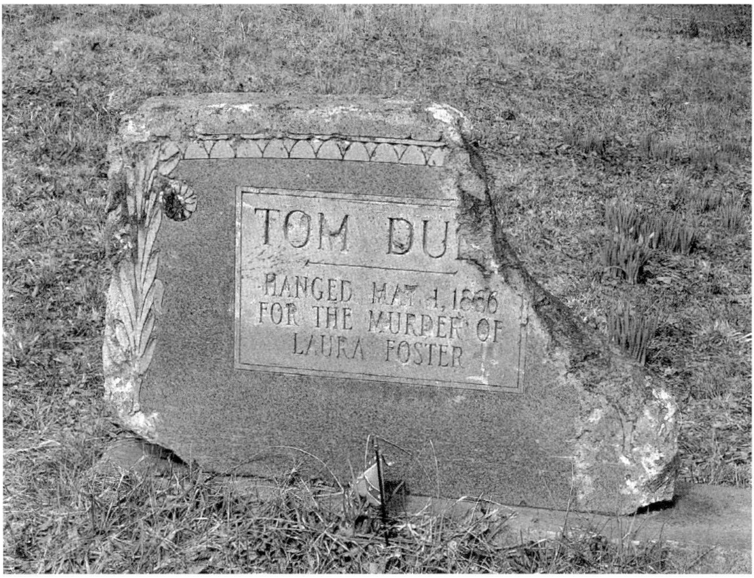

Tom Dooley's grave marker has been damaged by souvenir hunters. Note the incorrect date of his death on the stone.

THUMPER S BRANCH

Not long after Tom Dooley was buried, there was an old Irish peddler selling his wares from a push cart. He moved from house to house, selling such goods as needles and thread, soap and medicines of the day. It was getting late and the old peddler was tired. He decided to rest for the night and stopped to camp next to a small stream. Soon the peddler fell sound asleep.

Across the stream stood an old log house where a family lived. They got up early the next morning and went outside to do their morning chores. They looked across the stream and saw a strange sight. They rushed to the scene and found a push cart turned over and goods scattered everywhere. On the ground lay the peddler, dead. Someone had robbed and killed him during the night.

Since the peddler had no known home or friends, the family assisted with the burial and buried the man on a small creek within a short distance of their home. The following night, the family heard a strange thumping noise coming from the grave. The thumping noise resembled a heart beating and the family reasoned that the spirit had returned to find out who murdered the Irish peddler. The old family home and exact site of the grave have been lost from record. However, if you go up Tom Dooley Road at night, when you get to Thumper's Branch, don't be surprised if you hear the "thump, thump, thump." It's the old peddler's spirit still looking for his killers.

CHAPTER 7

GHOSTS OF THE SMITHEY HOTEL

NIKARD B. SMITHEY

The founder of Smithey's Stores, N.B. Smithey, was born on August 11, 1880. He was commonly known as Nike Smithey. Nike started out in the business selling beef to the people of the Wilkesboro community. Later he operated a small store in or near the old Chronicle building.

In 1906, Nike Smithey borrowed $3,800—which, according to many accounts, was the only money that he borrowed in his life—to purchase the Wilkesboro Hotel building. The former Wilkesboro Hotel was constructed in 1891 and had fallen on non-profitable times. Nike and his wife, Hattie from Catawba County, operated Smithey Hotel and Smithey Department Store chain for nearly half a century.

Frequently going north, Mr. Smithey would make long trips to New York and other large cities to buy large inventories of merchandise and bring it back to Wilkes and sell at bargain prices. Before the days of high-profile TV marketing, Smithey pioneered the use of a slogan: "Smithey's, the Great Bargain Givers." The old slogan remained on the Wilkesboro store building until the store was restored in 1966. After starting the Smithey's Store in Wilkesboro, Nike later expanded and bought a store in North Wilkesboro in 1928 and then started building chain stores in the northwest section of the state, Tennessee and Virginia. Smithey

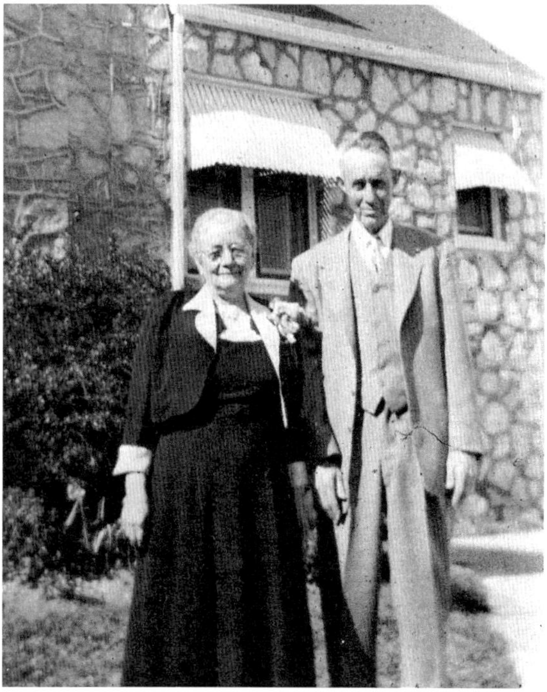

Hattie and Nike Smithey, the former owners of the Smithey Hotel and Store chain. *Courtesy of Dr. R Ernest Cohn.*

operated a total of seventeen Smithey's Stores by the time of his death on October 3, 1953.

Although Nike Smithey had little formal schooling, he was well versed in merchandising, banking and tax laws. In addition, he was often spotted constructing his own buildings, as he was good with construction, including his ability to lay rock, mortar and brick. Nike Smithey was a shrewd businessman. During one of his trips to New York, he told a man that he would be interested in buying all the items on a boxcar for $1,000. The man, who noticed that Smithey was dressed in bib overalls, said, "Sir, I would sell it to you if a person such as yourself could deliver $1,000." Smithey immediately produced the amount of money almost before the man could react and bought the boxcar full of merchandise on the spot.

Smithey did not to flaunt his wealth to the citizens of Wilkes County. He did buy a new car once a year but did not wish to appear too extravagant. He usually bought his car on a rainy day so that it would not appear too shiny. Once he bought a car on a clear day and paid a youngster a handsome fee of thirty-five cents to throw some mud on the car. Smithey always believed in buying in cash and didn't believe in using credit.

One thing that people consistently tell me about the Smitheys is that Nike and his family always reached out to fellow citizens in Wilkes County, even during the struggles of the Great Depression. I have heard many accounts where gentle kindness and generosity were the hallmarks of the Smitheys. In fact, my first summer job was working at Smithey's Department Store when I was a fifteen-year-old youngster growing up in Taylorsville, North Carolina. The store managers in Taylorsville were Marie, daughter of Nike Smithey, and her husband, Mr. G.M. Kirtpatrick. The Smitheys also ran a cafeteria in the basement of the department store. In fact, several of the Smithey's Stores contained cafés. To dine there was a treat! I remember well my first "liver-mush sandwich" and "Smithey Burger." The Smithey café contributed to my very first weight gain experience as a youngster.

Nike Smithey passed away in his sleep in September 1953. Citizens came in Cadillacs and pickup trucks alike to pay their last respects. Many lined the sidewalk for several blocks in order to honor their fallen friend, community leader and businessman. The family continued to run the Smithey Hotel and seventeen department stores for many years. The Smithey Hotel building in Wilkesboro was added to the National Register of Historical Places in 1982.

In the early 1990s, the Smithey Hotel was sold to Dr. R. Ernest Cohn, a chiropractor, medical doctor and local businessman. Dr. Cohn and his wife Sue decided to renovate the building and restore it to the style of the late Victorian period. They soon had it in much better shape than it had been in for a number of years. The Smithey Hotel is divided into three floors and a basement. Historically, the main level was used for the Smithey's Department Store, a meat market and the post office, while the second floor was occupied by the Smithey family and also included the dining room and kitchen. The third floor was the floor used for the motel guests and the basement level had dirt floors and served as the town's barbershop.

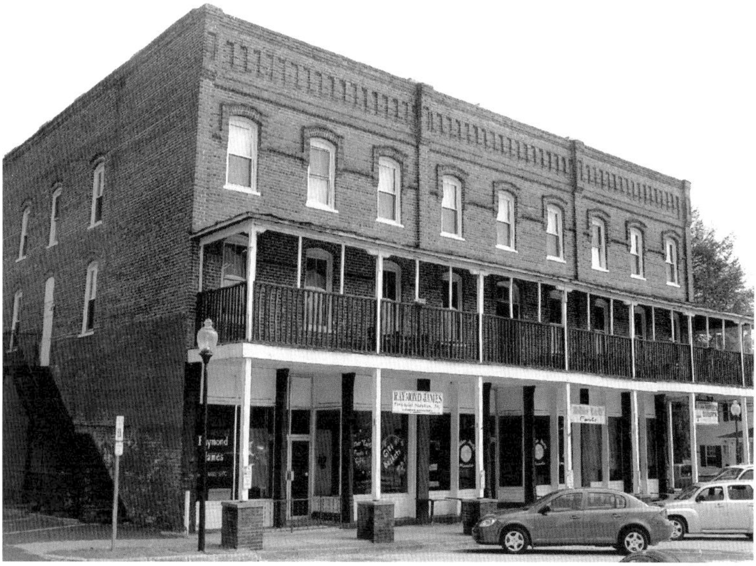

The Smithey Hotel, built in 1881 in the heart of Wilkesboro, was the home of Nike and Hattie Smithey for nearly half a century.

The Cohns operated Mother Earth Foods and the Tory Oak Restaurant. Today, Dooley's Grill and Tavern is on the first floor. Dooley's is a popular spot in the evenings and is a must-see when visiting downtown Wilkesboro. In both Dooley's Grill and Mother Earth Foods, a large collection of historic photographs fills the walls. There are photos showing Wilkesboro in the days of dirt streets, hitching posts and horses. The photos show townspeople as they appeared in clothing of much earlier times in history. Included in the collection are pictures of Nike and Hattie Smithey. It is a beautiful building with a vivid past. Another interesting fact is that auto racing had its roots in the hotel building when "Grand National Racing" began in the late 1940s. The forefathers of the modern sport NASCAR met at the Smithey Hotel and laid out the plans of the sport we know today.

As soon as the Tory Oak Restaurant and other businesses opened in the mid-1990s, stories of very strange happenings began to be reported. In those first few weeks and months that the Smithey Hotel's new owners opened their businesses, various sounds were heard. From the Mother Earth Foods, people could hear what they thought were the sounds of running children on the second floor. The workers say that people trying to see the ghosts almost never have an encounter but that those engaged in routine duties are much more likely to have an "experience."

AUTHOR'S NOTE: The outdoor drama *Moonshine and Thunder*, which runs annually during summers at Fort Hamby Park at W. Kerr Scott Reservoir, is highly recommended. The play was written by Karen Reynolds and is a very powerful and compelling production.

SOUNDS OF RUNNING CHILDREN

Historical details seem to relate to many experiences in the building. Joseph from Josephs of Wilkes, a local florist, reported that he could hear the sounds of fast feet running up and down the hallway and staircase. He assumed that it was Sue Cohn's six-year-old son and a friend playing. But when Sue was asked, Joseph found that her son was not there that day. On many other occasions, restaurant staff have heard sounds of people walking briskly up and down the third-floor steps.

Some believe that this can be attributed to an incident that happened in the early 1900s. A young boy was injured by burns from playing with fireworks on the Fourth of July. He was brought to the hotel for medical attention but did not survive the injuries. It is theorized that the spirit of the boy still continues to run and play on the third floor of the Smithey Hotel.

BERTHA BELL, THE COUNTY HEALTH NURSE

Some say her spirit still haunts the old hotel. Soon after the Tory Oak Restaurant opened for business, waiters and waitresses began noticing the appearance of an out-of-place visitor who seemed to come into view as the swinging doors would open and close in the doorway passage connecting the kitchen to the dining room on the second floor of the Smithey Hotel. The apparition has been described as a middle-aged woman with a thick figure, wearing a dark blue pleated dress with a white collar, thick nylon stockings and large-heeled and almost square-toed black shoes. The woman apparently has her hair gathered into a bun and appears with a rather stern and serious countenance. Following interviews from individuals who were familiar with the history of the old Smithey Hotel, the description nearly perfectly fits Bertha Bell, who was a tenant in the building for over twenty years as she worked for Wilkes County schools as a school nurse.

Those who remember her recall that she would drive up in an old black car carrying a black leather bag that contained nursing supplies. The students were very frightened of her because she administered shots. In fact, Bertha no doubt gave shots to thousands of students over her course of occupation. The thought of Bertha Bell with a syringe in hand was just about enough to cause childhood nightmares, especially if you were a student in the era from the late 1930s to the late 1940s.

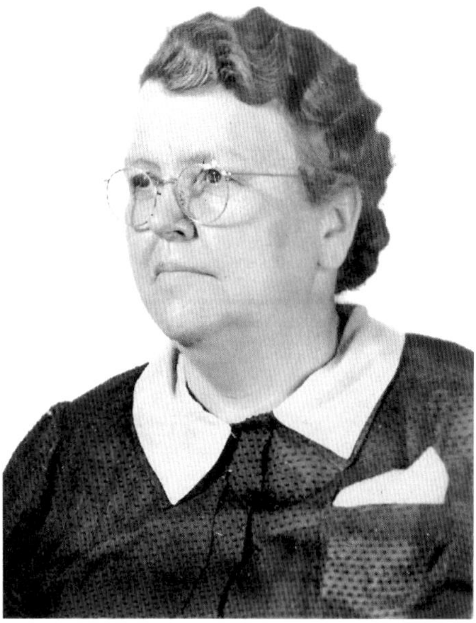

Bertha Bell served as the county school nurse for over twenty-five years. *Courtesy of Marilyn Payne, Wilkes Heritage Museum.*

Bertha Bell worked under Dr. Eller in the 1940s from his office in the Old Courthouse (now the Wilkes Heritage Museum). In looking at the old photographs, Ms. Bell indeed fits the description described by the Tory Oak waiters. Bertha Bell lived on the third floor of the hotel, which was the floor that the guests stayed in when the building was used as a hotel during its golden era. Bertha Bell was a common fixture, as she roomed there for many years while working for the school system.

If you have occasion to dine in the Smithey Hotel or visit it during one of the ghost tours, be on the lookout. You might just spot Bertha Bell roaming the halls or on the other side of one of the swinging doors. If you have children on the tour, you can even ask, "Are any of you guys in need of inoculations?" Imagine the full-figure image of Bertha Bell standing there with a syringe ready to administer your shots!

Some also say that they see a shadow of a lady standing behind the opaque door near the rear of the kitchen area on the second floor. Accounts vary, but this ghost has been reported to be standing so as to display its profile through the dense glass. When the door is opened and one looks behind the door, the person disappears.

The Lady Who Admires Art

Ron and Sue Cohn, in their renovations of the Smithey Hotel, hired a lady from California to do a late nineteenth-century mural on the high, arched oval hallway ceiling located at the top of the staircase that leads to the second floor. The painting was to be a Victorian design. The California-based painter was not successful in painting in the style of the period and was let go from her job (her attempts resulted in more modern interpretations). Despite her inability to complete the work, she provided a strange account. As she painted lying on her back while positioned on scaffolding, she observed a woman standing in a long, flowing evening gown, reminiscent of the 1920s. The mysterious figure watched quietly as she painted the ceiling mural.

After the first painter left, a mother and her son from Wilkes County were hired to complete the *Scene of the Four Angels*, which depicts the

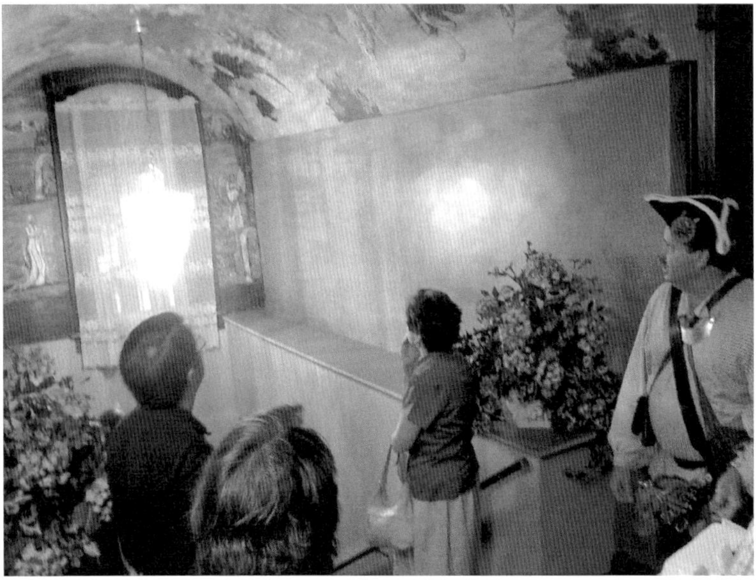

A ghost tour in the Smithey Hotel makes a stop at the "Scene of the Four Angels." *Photo by Donna Absher.*

stages of life from conception to death. On several occasions, the second couple reported the same apparition—a woman watching them paint the scene. The woman never talked but watched as the couple painted. Again, she was described as dressed in a beautiful, flowing evening gown. The woman appeared to almost float above the floor at the base of the steps. It was most interesting that neither the first nor second painters spoke to one another yet they described the same appearance of the lady apparition.

THE HELPFUL WAITRESS

Soon after the Tory Oak Restaurant opened, the layout of the restaurant was set in a formal late Victorian–style table setting, complete with fine china and silverware. One afternoon, a waitress was setting a table when she heard a woman's voice behind her say, "There are spoons missing." She glanced behind her, expecting to see Sue Cohn, but nobody was there. When she looked down at the table setting, indeed, a couple of spoons were missing. She continued to yet another table and the experience was repeated a second time. The voice again said, "I told you that the spoons are missing." Again the waitress turned around to see who was behind her and saw no one.

The young waitress then bolted, running quickly to the kitchen to see if someone was there or knew something of the command to replace missing spoons. She found Sue Cohn busy working in the kitchen. She asked Sue, "This may sound strange, but did you just ask me about missing spoons?" Sue answered, "I haven't left the kitchen." After learning of this account of the helpful ghost, Sue looked at the waitress in astonishment.

In the following months, other waitresses reported that table settings could be set up incorrectly and when waitresses would return, they would find the silverware in their proper placement. When Hattie Smithey ("Mrs. Hattie" or "Mrs. Smithey," as the staff sometimes called her) had worked around the hotel kitchen, it was known that she was a stickler for everything being just right and in its place. Mrs. Smithey was well aware of the correct table setting of the day, with specific locations for the main fork and salad fork, and knife placement being exactly correct with no deviations. It was known that Mrs. Hattie would have been quick to correct or fix an incorrect table setting.

Could it be? Could it be that still, this many years later, Hattie Smithey is still roaming the dining room in the Smithey Hotel? Is it possible that Mrs. Hattie is meticulously checking to see if everything is "just so" in her dining room and, on occasion, correcting any layout of the silverware table settings that are incorrectly placed by a waiter or waitress?

The Man with the Keys

The Tory Oak Restaurant was designed in a manner that further accents the Victorian style of the building. The bedrooms of the second floor were easily converted to dining rooms by the Cohns.

In the mid-1990s, a couple from Statesville, North Carolina, was dining in the Blue Room of the Tory Oak Restaurant, which is on the second floor and just down the hallway from the main dining room. This couple knew nothing of the history of Nike Smithey and nothing about the history of the Smithey Hotel. The waiter took the couple's order and then retired to the kitchen with order in hand. Suddenly, the waiter heard a scream from the Blue Room and hurried to see what the problem was. Upon checking into the situation, the waiter, Tim, found out that the couple was shaken by what they had seen. The couple took turns exchanging their descriptions and often interrupting each other as they described an almost unbelievable sight.

After regaining their composure, the Statesville couple indicated that they had seen a man standing in the threshold of the door at the hallway entrance to the Blue Room. The man was dressed in old-fashioned business attire, wearing a long black suit, an older-styled hat and carrying a heavy set of skeleton keys. The man with the keys stood in the Blue Room doorway attempting to open or lock a door. They said the man was very tall and stood out like a person out of history books, like the effect of seeing Abraham Lincoln in a modern place.

A little later that evening, when they finished dinner, the couple asked to visit Mother Earth Foods. Tim invited the couple to look at the excellent display of historic photos on the wall. After gazing at a number of photos, the couple then froze as they both pointed to a photo of Nike Smithey, previous store owner from 1906 until 1953. They said, collectively, "That's him, that's the man with the keys!" There was only one problem—Nike Smithey had been dead for over forty years!

It's an interesting fact that the Blue Room and the room immediately across the hall were once the childhood bedrooms of Nike Smithey's two daughters, Margaret and Marie. Mr. Smithey routinely checked on his daughters every night and locked the doors. The Smithey Hotel was a public place, and security was an issue. The Blue Room was Margaret's room while the room across the hall was where Marie slept. The hotel rooms to this day still contain the same doors and keyholes used by Nike Smithey for nearly half a century. Even the original molding and drop windows above the doors are in place. The drop windows were used to increase air flow on hot, sticky summer days.

On other occasions, other workers and people using the restaurant have reported the same encounter. One day, another one of the waiters asked how many men would be at a table that he was assigned to serve in the Blue Room. He was surprised when he was told that there was just one, for he had seen two men at the door. Curiously, he noticed that one of the men (the one not seated) was holding an old-fashioned set of keys, nervously jostling them at the threshold of the hallway. This was exactly the same position as described in the above account. Later, the waiter also identified the man by the picture of Mr. Nike Smithey and also stated, "That's the man I saw with the keys!"

Too Much to Drink

One evening a man who was enjoying the evening at Dooley's had a little too much to drink. Seth Cohn, operator of Dooley's and the son of Dr. Cohn, allowed the young man to sleep it off in a room on the second floor of the Smithey Hotel.

The next morning, the man awoke and recounted to Seth Cohn an experience that he had had during the night. He reported that an elderly woman with gray hair in a wheelchair approached him in a conversation. At some point in the conversation, she counseled the man on the overuse of alcohol.

Mrs. Hattie Smithey had lived to reach 104 years of age and spent the last few years of her life in an old wicker wheelchair, which the Cohns still have. It was also known that she frowned upon rowdy activity such as carousing and drinking. One story that emerged is that former Alcohol, Tax and Firearms (ATF) officer, Sam Cabe, for years kept a copper still in his room for his private use. The word was that Mrs. Smithey never was successful in catching Sam with the liquor and his small still. Some have said that maybe Mrs. Smithey is still looking for the liquor still, an act that she may have repeated many times in her life.

Nike Smithey's personal living quarters were a two-room suite at the end of the hall on the second floor, facing the Old Wilkes County Courthouse. Mr. Smithey used to look out onto the lawn of the Old Courthouse and watch people come and go to execute legal and civil functions during the daytime. Today this room is the Tory Oak bar. Today's existing English pub–styled wooden bar was handcrafted for Dr. Cohn by carpenter Bobby Jones, who spent six months restoring just this one room. The solid oak bar contains old walnut wood carvings on the side that were found in a wooden trunk belonging to Mr. Smithey. Most people don't know that the large dining room on the second floor was the site where Mr. Smithey lay in state at his funeral in 1953.

The Instant Hitchhiker

In yet another bizarre story, some people have reported an uninvited hitchhiker who shows up in the backseat of their vehicle when they pass in front of the Smithey Hotel on East Main Street. In the summer of 2004, actors Matt and Mickey Minton were driving through Wilkesboro one night from Benton Hall following a showing of *Tom Dooley, a Wilkes County Legend*, when they observed a strange, unannounced visitor suddenly riding in the backseat of the van. The van's doors were locked, as most vehicles nowadays lock automatically after reaching a certain speed. The female backseat rider was described as an old prim and proper lady sitting in the middle of the backseat. Her face seemed to bear a content smile as she looked straight ahead. The lady did not talk but had her hands on her purse and displayed a very upright posture and alert appearance. When Matt and Mickey were later shown a book of pictures of the Smithey women, they pointed out the picture of Mrs. Hattie Smithey as resembling the woman they saw in the van. When you pass the old hotel on East Main Street in downtown Wilkesboro, you may want to check your rearview mirror. You may have a hitchhiker aboard!

Lights Out in the Basement

One Halloween night in the late 1990s, the Cohns' son Seth was playing with a Ouija Board in the basement of the Smithey Hotel with friends when suddenly the lights went completely out. The boys fled in panic out of the basement, up the stairs and into the parking lot. Although the lights on the bottom floor were all on the same circuit, the lights were only off in the basement room. Later that evening, the Cohns drove by to discover that the lights were back on!

On another occasion, Sue's teenage son and some of his fellow band members were going into the basement of the building to practice their music. At that time, in order to enter the basement, you had to go through an outside cellar door like you see at Dorothy's aunt and uncle's house in *The Wizard of Oz* (stairs covered at a slant with a trapdoor that you pull up to enter). Two of the friends went up the stairs and outside to smoke cigarettes. When they went back to the basement door to go back inside, it was not only closed tightly—it was padlocked shut, and they could see through a crack in the door that the lights had gone out. This door has since been replaced with a normal door. Dr. Cohn was called that evening by his teenage sons. He arrived in "bed clothes," much to the teens' chagrin, and when Dr. Cohn went to inspect the door, it was unlocked. The door then swung open and the lights were back on in the basement.

CHAPTER 8

OTHER GHOSTS OF THE WILKESBOROS

FINLEY LAW OFFICE

A few years ago, Tammy Dinardo ran her Heritage Heirlooms gift shop immediately behind the Smithey Hotel and adjacent to the Wilkes Heritage Museum. Ms. Dinardo provided me with an amazing account of experiences that she had while operating at the old law office. Tammy came back from a weeklong vacation in June 2005 and discovered small collectable medicine bottles that had been positioned on the window ledge prior to departing for the vacation. Upon her return, some of the bottles were on the floor and some had been placed into odd patterns near her cash register. In addition, several pieces of furniture had been rearranged and were out of place. The fact that the very fragile bottles on the floor were not broken is strange indeed. The bottles were positioned into rather strange formations as if they had just dropped onto the floor.

Other strange occurrences have also taken place at the law office. Ms. Dinardo has heard footsteps when there is no one there. On another occasion, a customer came up the steps to enter the building and noticed that the rocking chairs on the front porch rocked on their own power. This is interesting as other buildings close by, such as the Johnson-Hubbard House, have also received reports of encounters with rocking chairs.

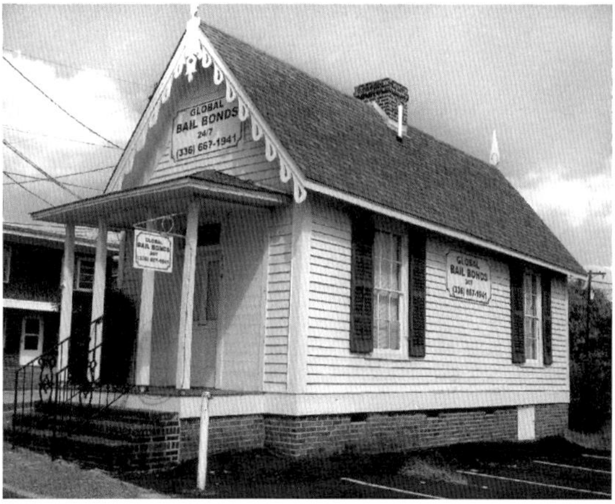

The Finley Law Office in Wilkesboro. *Courtesy of the Wilkes Heritage Museum.*

THE ENGLISH COTTAGE

The small gift shop known as the English Cottage is located less than a block south of the Wilkes County Heritage Museum (Old Wilkes County Courthouse). Only one building separates the English Cottage from the Smithey Hotel building. The owner of the English Cottage, Angela Gambill, is native to southern England and, as of this writing, runs the gift and antique shop. The gift shop is one of several gift shops that have sprung up in Wilkesboro in recent years with the development of downtown heritage tourism and the move toward revitalization. Gambill mentioned that she has been strangely locked out of the building before. The building locks were apparently locked from the inside with no one inside the building. (This is much like the story of the boys who were locked out of the basement of the Smithey Hotel on a Halloween night.)

Carol Black, formerly of Wilkes County and now residing in Alleghany County, North Carolina, tells about a strange story that happened a few years ago. Ms. Black (Ms. Stone at the time) had just moved here from the North and described herself as a "recovering Northerner." Carol found that when she drove past the Old Wilkes County Courthouse for the very first time, she sensed a strange connection to the old courthouse and just knew that she had seen the building before. Carol said, "I felt like I had been there before." Each time she would pass the building, the strange feeling of familiarity would transfix her momentarily.

Soon after moving into town to stay, Carol set up a massage practice in the Law and Bride Cottage (which is now the English Cottage), just a few yards away from the Smithey Hotel. The building needed a lot of work and sprucing up to get it ready to open. One day when she was rearranging and cleaning prior to opening her business, she was standing on a chair and painting over the front door. Suddenly she looked down and experienced something that she'll never forget.

Carol related, "Out of nowhere, it was as if I was in the same place but in another period of time. In one instant, I looked down and I was dressed in a long, brown, rough fabric skirt that women wore in the Great Depression. Then I looked at the interior of the room and walls and I saw hanging over the doors a bunch of herbs and roots drying in the morning sun. It was very brief and very real." It seemed that she had entered into a strange time warp and was briefly transposed to an earlier point in history, yet was in the same building. She thought to herself, this is very strange! Although totally strange to her, the experience was somehow very familiar. "I sensed a connection…I felt like I had been there before," said Carol.

A few days after the time warp incident at the cottage, she took a break from her new business and decided to attend a volleyball party with some friends. Another lady whom she met at the volleyball party also described herself as a "recovering Northerner." Oddly, after talking a good while, Carol felt like she knew the woman from a past time. The two were engaged in conversation and it's as if they could almost complete each other's sentences. Then out of the wild blue yonder, the lady asked Carol a question that surprised and astounded her. The other lady said, "Have you yet discovered that you've been here before?"

Other folks have noted a brief return to the past while frequenting the stores in downtown Wilkesboro. During one of the Old Wilkes Candlelight Ghost Tours, Jera Parsons, a person on the tour, said that recently when she was inside one of the antique stores on Main Street, she looked into a mirror and saw herself in eighteenth-century clothing!

JOHNSON—HUBBARD HOUSE

This house was built by Stephen Johnson in 1855 and then purchased by Julius Hubbard in 1885. The staircase runs, along with the upstairs bedroom ceilings, were painted with a technique known as "smoking pine torch" and are very beautiful and interesting to see. The upstairs bedrooms also contain elaborately carved crown molding. In addition, solid, one-piece banisters in the staircase required much effort and skill to manufacture. Mr. and Mrs. Bobby Phillips and their daughter, Allison Phillips, provided me with a guided tour through the Johnson-Hubbard House one day and I was amazed at the feeling of history that the house seems to possess.

Mr. and Mrs. Phillips recently ran a business in the old historic Johnson-Hubbard House. The Phillips family has experienced several very strange occurrences since occupying the historic building. Sounds of people moving about the house and staircase are common. In addition, recently Mrs. Phillips moved some old rocking chairs from the front porch to a small hallway entrance room on the second floor at the top of the staircase. Soon afterward, she heard sounds of a chair rocking. Upon investigation, and to her amazement, she found that the rocking chairs were rocking under their own power, with no wind or anybody visually occupying the chair. She could stop the chairs and return to the study, and strangely the chairs would again begin rocking. Today, the rockers have been returned to the front porch. Nowadays, visitors to downtown Wilkesboro can still see the two white rockers when they drive by the old Johnson-Hubbard House.

Kim Nichols tells the story of her grandmother, Hazel Nichols, who was born in 1904 and grew up in the Johnson-Hubbard House. She recounted some bizarre stories to her grandchildren regarding the old house. While the Hemphill family lived there around the early part of the twentieth century, very strange events took place. Hazel Nichols told of objects that moved on the walls or took the form of human faces. At times the faces tended to follow people as they moved from room to room. Apparitions were sighted and the presence of other people was often felt in the house. Objects such as wall fixtures and paintings would sometimes change form

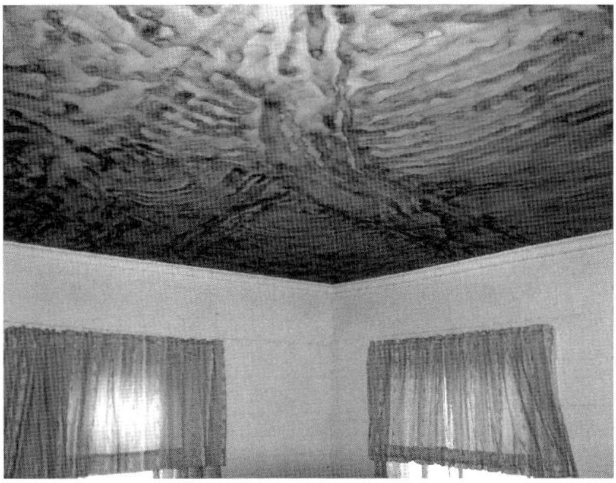

The interior ceiling of the Johnson-Hubbard House displays rare example of "pine torch painting."

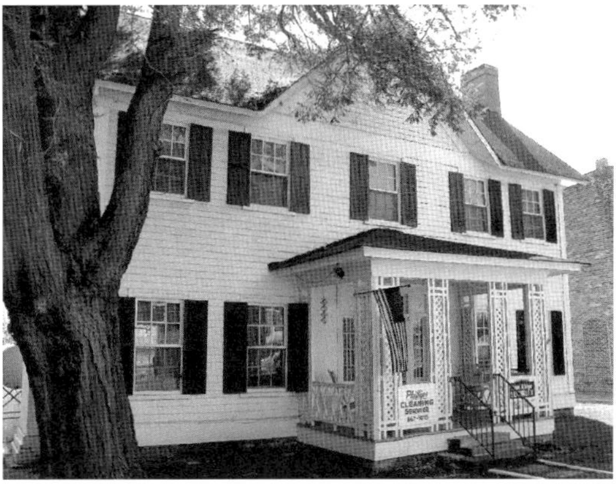

The Johnson-Hubbard House in Wilkesboro.

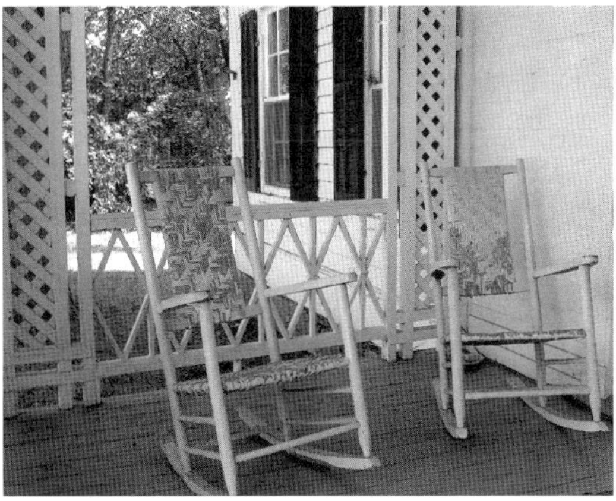

The rocking chairs on the front porch of the Johnson-Hubbard House are the subject of a strange account.

or move. It's striking that the stories recently told by the Phillips family are similar to the ones told a century ago.

Wilkesboro Presbyterian Chapel

The Presbyterian chapel in downtown Wilkesboro was built in 1849–50 and is one of the oldest standing Presbyterian churches in Western North Carolina. The church is still used as a chapel today and its beautiful columns and large windows display a rare glimpse of antebellum Wilkes. Around Christmastime, the candles in the windows and lights on the majestic columns are a beautiful sight. Presbyterianism was initially one of the most common churches among the Scotch-Irish who brought the "Scottish Kirk" from Ulster to America in the early 1700s. Though later giving in to the popularity of the Baptists and Methodists, the Presbyterian denomination was certainly dominant among the first Scotch-Irish settlers.

Steve Snipes, the minister, saw me with a group as I walked by the Presbyterian chapel one evening recently. That night, I had an especially large group trailing behind me en route to the cemetery. The reverend appeared amused and then yelled out, "Looks like I need to borrow something that you are using to get my attendance up on Sunday mornings!"

Benton Hall

Actors and staff at Benton Hall in North Wilkesboro, North Carolina, say that the building is haunted. Numerous accounts have been reported of strange noises and other kinds of things that seem to occur in the old historic building. Benton Hall is located at 300 D Street in North Wilkesboro and was once the site of North Wilkesboro Elementary School. In the late 1990s, Wilkes Playmakers undertook the management and renovation of the building and converted it into a beautiful playhouse. The building today is also used for many purposes, including Tiffany's Place

Teen Center, and for meetings, social events, plays and musicals. Wilkes Playmakers has been a part of Wilkes County theatre and North Carolina community theatre since 1990. Today the entity is divided into three organizations—Wilkes Playmakers, Benton Hall, Inc., and Tiffany's.

Karen Reynolds, the executive director of Benton Hall, has related several occurrences in the building. She indicated that on several occasions, the sounds of children (described as if they were children talking in a classroom in large numbers) have been heard. Each time, when investigated, no children were present in the building. Ghost tour guide Julie Mullis also confirmed this experience. When her Wilkes Community College students were visiting backstage of the theatre, they heard sounds of unsupervised children playing and laughing in the main auditorium. When they checked, no children were in the room or even in Benton Hall.

Jeremiah Greer and his team of paranormal investigators recently conducted an investigation there. Greer pointed to the past history of the building. He thinks that the fact that Benton Hall was once a school certainly adds interest to claims of talking or playing children. During their investigation, Greer and his team recorded an EVP that sounded like guitar music being played. It's known that such music has been played in Benton Hall many times over the years.

Others working in Benton Hall late at night report feeling a strange presence in the building, especially in some of the locations such as a back entrance stairway to the auditorium and in the Green Room, which is a backstage area. Both Julie Mullis and Heather Osborne reported smelling the very fragrant smell of cloves in the Green Room. I spent a couple of summers at Benton Hall in the *Tom Dooley* show. I was in the building alone on a couple of occasions and do remember occasionally hearing unusual sounds of other people in the building in ways previously described. People often hear their name called to find out that nobody is in the building.

Heather Osborne told me about an astonishing experience that she had at Benton Hall. Back in 2002, following one of the *Tom Dooley* rehearsals, different actors were invited to reenact the Tom Dooley hanging scene. Each person got a chance to put on the

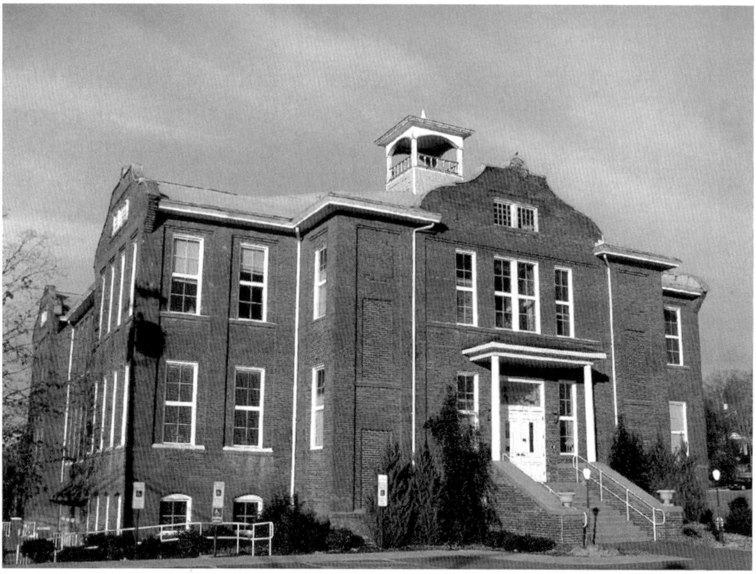

Benton Hall, once an old schoolhouse, is now a home for plays and a youth center that both entertains and serves the public.

safety harness and stand beneath the gallows, allowing themselves to harmlessly swing as a trapdoor was released. This way, they could simulate or reenact the hanging of Tom Dooley. For Heather, the event turned strange. When the noose was placed around her neck, she suddenly felt transposed to a different time and place. She was outdoors and could feel the wind and rays of sunshine. She could hear crowd noise and felt people push her as if a mob was rushing her toward the gallows. When she approached the gallows, she remembered hearing a man's voice: "Do you have any last words?" In the next moment, the trapdoor was released and the sequence seemed to suddenly be in slow motion. Time seemed to freeze. Then all went black for a brief instant, which seemed much longer. When Heather was harmlessly released, she appeared dazed and the other actors came up to her and said, "Are you all right?" Heather answered back, "Hey everybody, this was way too scary!" Heather had experienced a strange and frightening recreation of a hanging that seemed much too real.

Daddy's Ghost

Danny Reavis, a Wilkes Heritage Museum volunteer tour guide, relates a story in which a ghost apparently moved with the bedroom furniture when the furniture was moved to a house in North Wilkesboro. Reavis courted a young woman in Wilkes County who had moved here from the small town of Burnsville in Yancey County. Soon the couple was engaged to be married and a trip to Burnsville was arranged for Danny to meet his future mother-in-law. Hesitant at first, the future wife finally consented to the trip back home to meet her mother.

During the night, Danny slept in the guest bedroom that was once the bedroom of his fiancée's father. It was late March, so Danny closed the door and tightly pulled the covers up to stay warm during the evening. About 2:00 a.m., Danny awoke to the sounds of an opening bedroom door. After hearing the door creep open, he rose and checked the door to find that no one was there. Again at 3:00 a.m., the event repeated itself. And yet again at 4:00 a.m. he was awakened to the sounds of a creaking door. Once more, no one was there.

The next morning, Danny told his soon-to-be mother-in-law and fiancée about the strange event of the door opening during the previous night. They replied, "Oh, it's just Daddy's ghost paying you a visit. It happens all the time!" It turned out that in 1970, the fiancée's father had indeed shot himself in the mouth with a 30.06 rifle and blew off most of his head. Bone fragments of the grisly shooting were still embedded in the headboard of the old bed where the suicide occurred.

In spite of the strange encounter with "Daddy's ghost," the couple married and soon spent the night in the old house again. That night, they were sleeping in Daddy's bed when they were awakened by a loud crash at about 3:00 a.m. After turning on the lights, they discovered that several family pictures lying on a dresser had strangely fallen forward as if pushed by something. The new bride said, "It's only Daddy, you'll get used to it!"

The mother-in-law passed away in 2001 and the Reavis couple inherited the infamous bed suit that had been in the house in

Burnsville. The bed was moved to the Reavis residence in North Wilkesboro. When someone sleeps over for the evening, they notice that the doors open and close, things fall off the walls and noises are difficult to explain. Rest assured, it's just daddy's ghost. Nothing bad has really happened—at least not yet.

THE SWEEPING LADY

Across the road from the Presbyterian chapel and near several law offices on East Main Street in Wilkesboro, several people have reported what they call "the sweeping lady." Passing motorists have reported that a lady sometimes appears at dusk, dressed in early twentieth-century clothing, sweeping the yards in town. At the turn of the century, it was a common practice to sweep yards. Before the advent of lawn mowers, lawn maintenance was carried out by raking and sweeping dirt lawns. Grass lawns came later with the advent of gasoline-powered mowers.

It was once considered a good deed to rake someone's yard. When a person experienced hard times, family sickness or death, as an act of kindness, people would sweep their neighbors' yard. Evidently, there lived a woman in the late nineteenth century who was especially diligent in raking yards. She was described as a person with nearly endless energy and apparently could not rest until all in need had their yards raked. Apparently, she is still repeating the act of kindness and is still sweeping the yards in downtown Wilkesboro.

CHAPTER 9

GHOSTS IN THE HOLLOWS

MISTS ON THE MOUNTAIN

There was a lady who lived in the late 1800s near the Watauga/Wilkes County line in the Maple Springs community. Like most of her family, she was very superstitious and often expressed anguish and fear that her house was constructed on top of an old graveyard. It was noted that many visitors who slept in the old house reported moaning sounds when they spent the night. Some of the victims buried in the graves beneath the house had died violent deaths. Also, it was known that the field of medicine at that point in history was more limited in success and a higher mortality occurred from disease, injury and childbirth.

One particular story was especially disturbing. Buried beneath the house were a mother and two twins who all died in a failed childbirth a few years prior to the lady's house being built over the graveyard. The mother was buried with the twins cradled in her arms.

Some residents of Maple Springs still report that they see the same apparition that the superstitious lady first reported back in 1880. Many times late in the evening before dark, fog would form from the house above the graveyard and then roll down the hollow like a round ball. When the ball of fog reached the end of the hollow, the fog would take the form of a mother cradling two babies in her arms. The spirit is thought to be upset that her grave was disturbed by the house built over it and she will not rest until the house is torn down.

The Ghosts of the Green Park Inn

The watershed of the Yadkin River begins at a resort in Blowing Rock known as the Green Park Inn. Situated at an altitude of 4,300 feet, the summer retreat has greeted the very wealthy and even past presidents. Its history goes back more than 125 years and was the site of a Civil War stockade. Room 318 was supposed to be the room where once a jilted bride committed suicide.

Today, the Green Park Inn has been the site of ghost investigations and even a paranormal conference. The inn is so notoriously haunted that the hotel keeps a "ghost register" at the front desk so visitors can record their paranormal encounters. Reports range from the sounds of laughter and footsteps coming from invisible children to mysterious knocks, door openings and cold spots. Those visitors not interested in the haunts may enjoy the relaxing pace, abundant golf courses and mountain scenery.

The Devil Dog of Purlear

Dangerous wild animals have been reported along the Yadkin River Valley ever since the Moravian survey party passed through the region in the fall of 1752. The early settlers were mindful that wolves, mountain lions and bears could steal their food, kill their livestock and even pose a threat to their own safety.

For several generations in the community of Purlear, reports described a large, wild, black dog that roamed the countryside and created havoc, frightening people out of their wits. Tradition says that this dog was raised from a litter of pups at a place called "Devil's Staircase" in Ashe County. Devil's Staircase is a man-made rock formation caused by blasting during railroad construction in the early 1900s. This formation of giant steps is located in a narrow rocky gorge between West Jefferson and Lansing, North Carolina. Devil's Staircase is reported to be haunted.

Apparently, a pup wondered off from the litter and was picked up by a man driving a wagon who had just delivered a load of moonshine to Lansing and was returning to Wilkes. The dog found its new home in Purlear. It was raised around a moonshine still and became a very effective and feared guard dog. Not everyone in the community approved of the dog, and apparently the animal was poisoned by an irate neighbor. Some believe that today the dog's spirit still guards the old moonshine still locations near Purlear.

A few years after the dog died from poisoning, Will Church was hauling a wagonload of lumber with a team of mules near the New Hope Baptist Church in Purlear. He was beside the mules when he looked up and saw a huge black dog charging down the road. He picked up a whip and attempted to hold the dog at bay. The dog looked at Church, growled and displayed his teeth in a very threatening way. Church noticed something very bizarre in this aggressive and dangerous-looking beast. He observed that the eyes of the creature had turned an intense red, as if fueled by burning coals. As he reached for a weapon to subdue the dog, suddenly it vanished into thin air. A few minutes later, another man by the name of Mr. Griffin came along the wagon road. Church quivered and said with a shaky voice, "Don't believe you ought to go that way, I just saw the devil dog of Purlear!"

Since that day, many people have reported unexplained sounds in the backwoods of the Purlear community. Still others have reported a dog with eyes of burning brimstone displaying frighteningly aggressive behavior. If you go there, especially near any location of old moonshine stills, be on the lookout for the devil dog.

GRAVITY HILL

From the Thurmond community, near the county line of Wilkes and Surry, comes a story that defies gravity. If you drive on U.S. Highway 21 north of State Road, you will come onto a road that is an older route of Highway 21. If a person drives down the road, turns the car around and heads back in the direction of Highway 21, he can stop the car, put it in neutral and the car will appear as if it is coasting up a slight incline. Many people have made this drive to the old road to try it for themselves. I've talked to a number of people who are completely convinced, almost to the point of

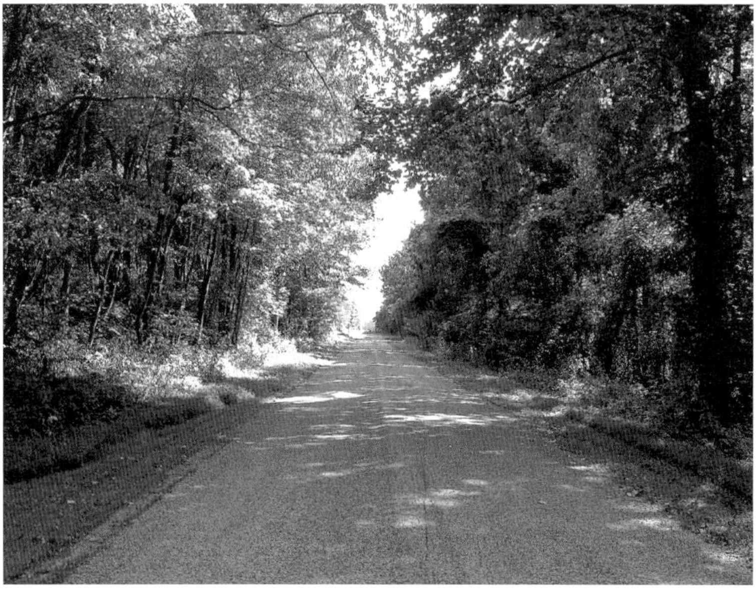

Gravity Hill, where gravity seems to play tricks.

argument, that gravity is being defied at Gravity Hill. I decided to give it the *Myth Buster* test. A year or so ago, I drove to Gravity Hill to try it myself. I turned the car around and put the car in neutral. Disbelief turned into astonishment! Oddly, I found that the lay of the land along the road at that point does indeed create the illusion that you are climbing a slight hill.

Accounts indicate that at the terminus of the road that dead-ends near a section of houses, a terrible tragedy took place many years ago. Apparently, a murder-suicide resulted in the loss of an entire family. Some accounts even say that if you sprinkle dust on your car window, fingerprints form on the glass to prove that young children, attempting to escape the tragedy, push the car uphill in the direction of U.S. Highway 21.

THE GHOSTS OF ELKIN CREEK VINEYARD

Mark Green, the owner of Elkin Creek Vineyard, on the outskirts of Elkin, North Carolina, has reported a number of very interesting events that have led him to believe that the old gristmill and grounds adjacent to his vineyard and restaurant are haunted. A few years ago, Green, a graduate of Wake Forest and the oenological and viticulture program at Surry Community College, after finding success as a banker and small business owner, cast his lot as a restaurateur and winemaker. After purchasing the century-old mill, he and his wife planted the vineyard and built the winery/restaurant with help from a few friends and his five children.

Green was enchanted with the beautiful cool waters of Big Elkin Creek as it tumbled by the gristmill site. The old mill building still stands as a reminder of the days when harnessing nature's power meant utilizing the force of falling water to turn a large wheel. The water wheel, through a series of pulleys and belts, turned large millstones that ground grain into flour. That flour was marketed

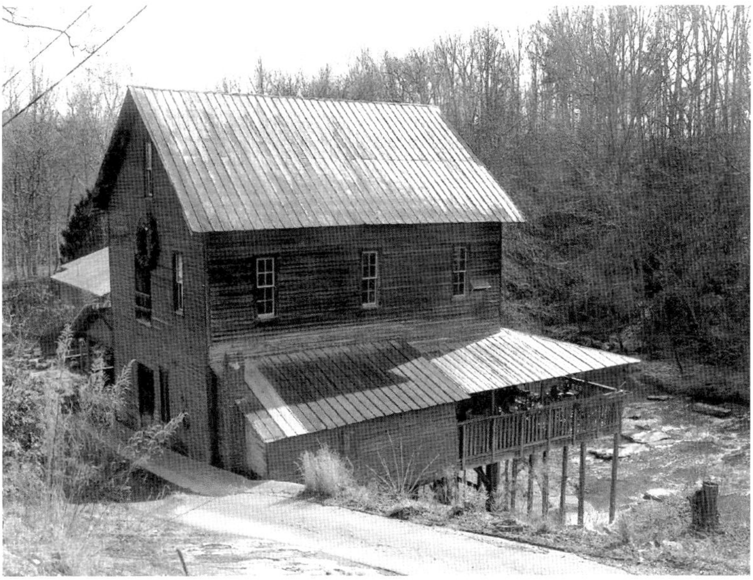

Historic Elkin Creek Mill is now the scene of a vineyard, winery and restaurant.

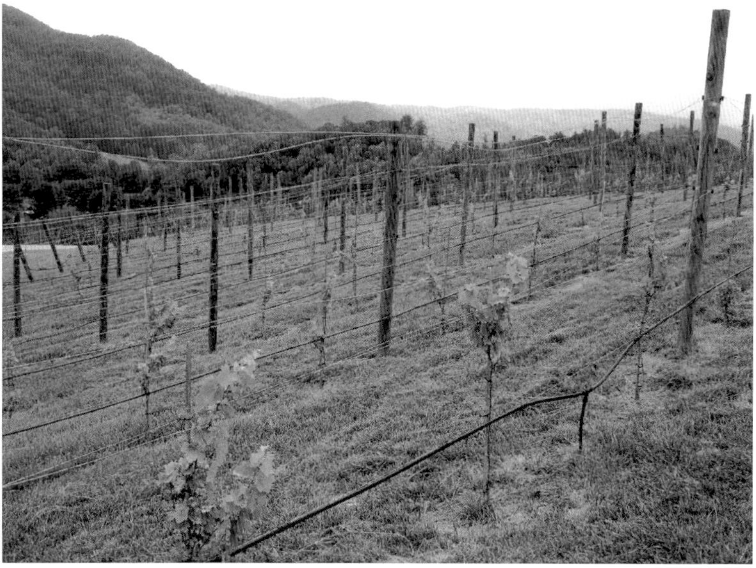

Benny Parsons Rendezvous Ridge Vineyards, named for NASCAR legend Benny Parsons, is one of over thirty vineyards located in the Yadkin Valley. *Courtesy of Benny Parsons Rendezvous Ridge Vineyards.*

to local residents and helped shape the early economy of the communities along the Yadkin Valley. Today, Elkin Creek shows flashes of the historic while showcasing the new. The new kids on the block are the region's wineries and vineyards.

The numerous vineyards and wineries in the area have created a destination in the upper Yadkin region of North Carolina, which is becoming one of the most exciting wine-growing regions in the United States. Nowadays, Green is occupied with the operation of his vineyard and restaurant, the Kitchen at Elkin Creek.

Previous owners and workers at the mill consistently reported strange happenings there. One tale was of a lady who had been grieving the loss of several close relatives. Gradually getting over her loss and rebuilding her life, she was preparing to marry a gentleman from Tennessee when she received news that he too had been killed in an auto accident. The lady became even more saddened and her grief was almost unbearable. She lingered in that depressed state for many days.

Sometime later, she was visited by a strange messenger. A bird alighted on the porch at the mill and seemed not to be afraid. As she looked closely at the bird, she noticed that its physical features and actions reminded her of her lost fiancé. The bird stayed for several days and somehow provided great comfort to the grieving lady. When the bird left, she suddenly felt a wonderful release and was no longer haunted by the intense grief that she previously had experienced. After reviewing bird identification books, she saw that the bird was fairly rare in the United States—that is, except in the one area in Tennessee where her lost fiancé was from.

Soon after Green began planting grapes and building his facilities, other strange events began to occur around the old mill site. Some of the workers noted that they often spotted a large man in bib overalls walking about the old gristmill, which is located just below the restaurant along the creek. A man fitting that description, a Mr. Adams or "McAdams," used to work at the mill until he became ill and passed away. It is thought that the man was so lonely that his spirit didn't want to leave his beloved work site. No doubt, in its heyday, the millers at Elkin Creek Mill were very industrious citizens and were deeply dedicated to their profession.

One of the most astonishing reports had to do with lights that seemed to turn on at the mill by some type of intelligence. For example, if Green were to leave for a few hours during the night and return, he often found that the lights in the old mill would be on when he came back in the evening hours.

One night Mark Green went down to the house to talk to his friend, the resident ghost of the mill. Although he didn't hear or see anything, Green reasoned with the ghost this way: "I know you want to be here, and I know that I want to be here as well. I don't have a problem with you staying, as long as you turn off the lights and help save on electric bills." From that point on, the lights have remained off when Mark Green returns during the evening hours. If you visit the Elkin Creek Vineyard today, you may see the old miller in overalls, but rest assured, Elkin Creek is operated primarily by the living!

THE CONFEDERATE SENTINELS OF ELKIN

The Yadkin Valley sent its share of soldiers off to fight in the Civil War. The grim side was that many of the area's young and able men were lost in that great conflict. The area around Elkin, North Carolina, was especially hit hard by those losses. The casualty list from the Battle of Gettysburg included a heavy number of Yadkin soldiers killed in the largest land battle on American soil to that date.

As word came to towns like Elkin following the Battle of Gettysburg, families were shocked and greatly saddened by these losses. Some communities lost as many as one third of their young men to that war. The horror of the Civil War and losses of the war were magnified by fears caused during General Stoneman's campaign during March 1865.

A tradition says that when Stoneman descended upon the Yadkin River, the ghosts of those lost Confederate soldiers from Elkin would stand sentinel at night in the windows of the houses in town. Apparently, the ghosts of the lost soldiers were concerned that the town would be burned by Stoneman and wished to console the town folks that all was well as they were standing guard. Confederate ghost sentinels have also been reported at other places in the valley, such as at the Elk Lodge in North Wilkesboro.

Today, when people drive by old houses during the evening hours, many say that they have spotted Confederate soldiers standing in the windows or in yards and driveways in town. Some are described as bearded men in Confederate uniforms, holding their Enfield rifles and reassuring the local folk that all is well.

AN ENCOUNTER AT A DROWNING SITE

On September 1, 1980, area newspapers reported the drowning of a nineteen-year-old lady from Wilkes County. The tragedy occurred in a swimming accident that took place at Wilkes County Park, which has since been renamed Fort Hamby Park. At about two o'clock in the afternoon on Saturday, August 30, the victim was swimming with two other female friends when they got into trouble. The young lady apparently swam out farther to rescue her struggling friends. After she successfully assisted the other two women from a deeper location in the water, the victim, tired, drifted to the deeper water and disappeared from view. Later that afternoon, rescuers found her body in about eight to ten feet of water. The tragedy greatly saddened the community, as the young and popular girl died that day.

Later on the evening of August 30, Jill Parsons and her date were returning from a high school evening social that had taken place earlier that evening in Boone, North Carolina. They were driving east on U.S. Highway 421 on a return trip to Wilkesboro when they decided to ride down by the lake "to watch the submarine races," a code meaning that they were going to hang out at the lake.

At around 11:00 p.m., the couple turned off the main highway and headed down to the entrance road leading to the recreation area where their friend had drowned earlier that afternoon. The night seemed innocent enough. With the car windows down, one could hear the fall katydids and other insects singing away in the night air. Nothing strange or odd was noticed. It was a typical warm summer night. The two knew nothing of the tragic event of their young friend that had happened earlier that afternoon.

As the couple drove along the road to a place near the swimming beach where the drowning had occurred, there, out of the darkness, they witnessed something that they would never forget. An eerie object came into full view in their headlight beams. It was the figure of a young woman floating across the road in front of them in what appeared to be a partly vaporized but clearly visible state. The woman was described as having long, flowing hair, and appeared to be drifting across the road with her toes pointed, dangling a few feet above the road surface. The apparition was plainly visible to both Jill and her boyfriend.

Jill Parsons was shocked at seeing this seemingly spiritual female body floating across the road. After a sleepless night, the next morning she reported this sighting to her mother, Judy Parsons, at the breakfast table. It was at this time that Jill Parsons learned the news that her friend had drowned in the waters near the old

Fort Hamby site. To be sure, this is an event that Jill Parsons will never forget.

The Man in Overalls

A man wearing overalls has appeared to a woman who resides in the Beacon Hill neighborhood in Wilkesboro. Beacon Hill is a more recent development and features very modern houses. The odd thing about this story is that the man wearing bib overalls seems to come from an earlier time. Apparently, the man leaves dimes lying around all over the house. He has been spotted in the house and outside in the yard. The lady also suggests that at times she can feel the strong presence of the man. Although the man never talks, she feels that he is trying to tell her something.

Years ago, men used to carry dimes around because lots of things cost ten cents. Back in the 1950s, several items cost ten cents. Some of these items may have included soft drinks, a plug of tobacco or the cost of a shoe shine. In Wilkes County, from the 1940s through the 1960s, overalls were commonly worn, especially among the farmers and timber cutters of the area. The appearance of the man in the overalls may indeed be related to someone who lived or worked near the location of the house in an earlier time.

CHAPTER 10

PLEASANT DREAMS

Conducting the ghost tours for the past few years has left a trail of memorable experiences. A lot of folks who have attended the ghost tours have written us back with additional stories of their own. We've had many great times around the campfires in an environment of storytelling and sharing of folk tales of the region.

One of the spinoff benefits of these ghost tours has been the new friends whom we've met in the process. The Southern Culture Class of Wilkes Community College has undertaken research projects of the stories and these projects have contributed to the interest in writing and historically related studies of area students.

We've had at least two groups conduct paranormal investigations at the Old Wilkes Jail, the Robert Cleveland House and the Brown-Cowles House and slave quarters in downtown Wilkesboro. EVP readings and orbs have been captured at some of these locations. In 2008, *Shadows in the Dark*, by Blog Talk Radio, did a twenty-four-hour live broadcast from the Smithey Hotel and featured a wide variety of interviews on paranormal and related subjects during the popular web-based broadcast.

So here we are near the end of the book. After taking you through some of our region's history and stories, I hope that you have enjoyed this step into the realm of folklore and ghost tales. I will end these chapters with the last two stops of the Candlelight Ghost Tours. Let us now go to the cemetery.

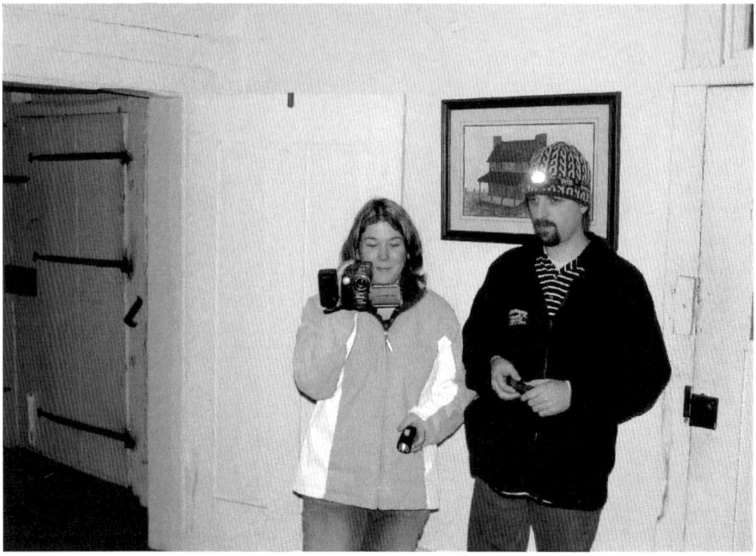

Paranormal investigators check for activity in the Old Wilkes Jail.

THE TOWN CEMETERY

The Wilkesboro Cemetery is an eerie place at night. When a person walks through, he will observe grave markers. Some are leaning and others are upright, while other monuments tower above the visitors. Graves in the Wilkesboro Town Cemetery date back as far as the American Revolution and there are slave graves that date to before the Civil War. In addition, several prominent citizens and political leaders are buried there.

The town cemetery is a favorite spot on the Candlelight Ghost Tours. It is there that tour guides share both the humorous and the morbid tales. Visitors are asked to recall the details of Mark Twain's famous novel, in which Tom Sawyer and Huck Finn took a blood oath and witnessed a murder in a cemetery. Many of our tour participants admit to visiting a graveyard at night and can identify with its scary side. In fact, ghost guide Heather Osborne, along with members of the Winston-Salem Paranormal Society, has photographed orbs while in the cemetery at night.

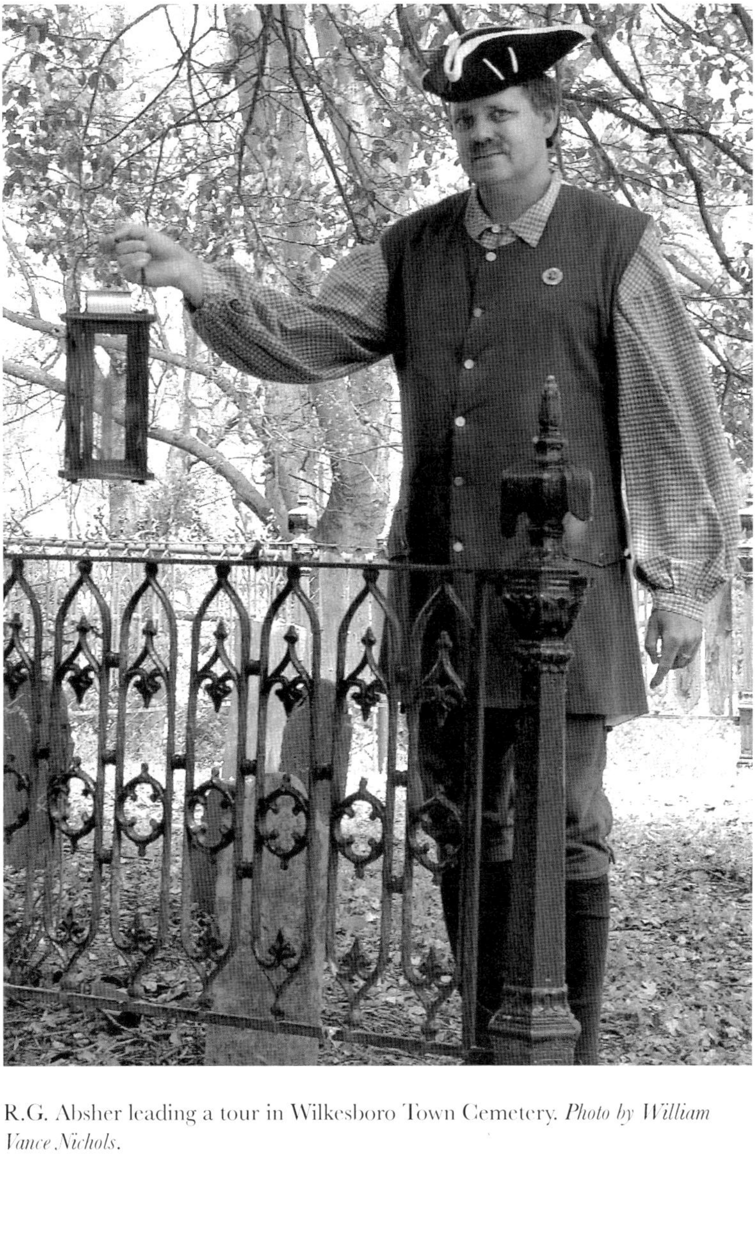

R.G. Absher leading a tour in Wilkesboro Town Cemetery. *Photo by William Vance Nichols.*

During a period of history that we ghost guides call "BF" (before formaldehyde), people had to handle the dead in such a manner as to prevent attack from wild animals that roamed the adjacent forests. The body could not be left unattended and had to be buried quickly in order to prevent it from being discovered and torn to pieces by wolves or other wild animals. Also, years ago, people were concerned about grave robberies, as some people would attempt to dig up graves to search for gold or valuables that were buried with the deceased.

Dr. Charles Gilreath, a chiropractor from Elkin, North Carolina, says that he is the only ghost guide who actually is old enough to have known the ghosts. One night I overheard Dr. Gilreath work with his tour group. "Do you folks know what happens to your body when you die? Did you know that your fingernails, hair and eyelashes continue to grow for some time? This will cause your appearance to look less than 'well groomed.' That is if you are lucky enough to be embalmed. If not, you will be consumed by the maggots in just a few days," said Dr. Gilreath.

Studies from the infamous "Body Farm" near Knoxville, Tennessee, allowed forensic scientists to determine time since death in investigations by studying the life cycle of the maggot. Persons can lose their skin to maggots and decomposition in as little as fifteen days. The body erodes and becomes just a skeleton in just a short amount of time.

A pattern of ghost experiences often occurs at battlefields, murder scenes and cemeteries. Old historic graveyards contain a lot of history if their residents could talk. Is it possible that they still can?

THE OLD HOOK ON THE CAR DOOR STORY

AUTHOR'S NOTE: This makes for a great story if you have a small metal hook that looks kind of like a pirate hook (used when a person lost an arm). Basically, the ghost guide stands behind a large tombstone with the tour participants on the other side. This allows the tour guide to set up the prop without revealing it. Then the guide tells the following tale:

In the 1950s, when the activity known as "car cruising" became popular, it became fashionable for young couples to park in cemeteries for the purpose of courting. Couples then began to mysteriously disappear at cemeteries, leaving an iron hook, like a pirates hook, as the only evidence. The hook would usually be left dangling on the car door handle following the disappearance of these young innocent couples. Following police investigation after investigation and line-up after line-up, investigations came up empty. The only evidence each and every time following the disappearance of a couple was the discovery of an ugly iron hook dangling from the car door.

The storyteller then delivers this statement: "Nobody, ladies and gentlemen, ever figured out who did the crime. The crime has gone unpunished and the culprit has gone free all this time. That is until—now!"

At this exact time, the ghost guide delivers the hook into full view of the shocked subjects. Most people will jump or scream. On one tour, a young boy took the bait so well that he fainted and hit the ground in shock! Indeed, nothing works better than the backdrop of a cemetery for telling scary ghost stories!

The Last Stop

We end our ghost tours in downtown Wilkesboro in front of the Smithey Hotel. At that point, we have the ghost participants focus on one of the windows as we stand there on East Main Street. The ghost guide then relates, "Through those windows lies a different tale and a unique story. Now ponder the possibility if you will. Most would agree that it's possible for a family to live in a facility for nearly half a century and carry on daily duties almost continuously, nearly twenty-four-seven, repeating routine preoccupation over and over in this old Victorian building. In some means not yet explained by science, by type of vortex or energy field, is it possible that some snapshot of activity, an entity, could make sound, produce smells, move objects, appear as from another time, make its presence known or even interact with the living?" The guide continues, "Is it is possible for people's spirits to somehow linger or return to a site or structure and interact with the living? It is possible that in the age of high-speed circuits, underground radar, digital devices and super computers some unexplained phenomena has yet to be discovered."

Is it possible for the restless to remain restless? Pleasant dreams!

CHAPTER 11

A FARMHOUSE IN GEORGIA

I will end this book the way I started it: by telling you about an experience that happened to me. The story goes back to 1978 to Reed Creek, a small rural community on the shores of Hartwell Lake, just north of Hartwell, Georgia. This is an experience that was my sole encounter to date with what I believe was a haunted house.

My friend Dan Page, who was a fellow park ranger for the U.S. Army Corps of Engineers at Hartwell Lake, and I drove past a large hayfield. Thc cnchanting scene came into full view. Our eyes opened widely when we saw the large Victorian farmhouse with a huge sweeping front porch. The house had a red tin roof, wooden gray siding and was flanked by a weeping willow tree on one side and a large chinaberry tree on the other. Behind the house was a long, gently sloping field that extended down to the shores of Hartwell Lake. "Wow!" we thought. "We can't wait to move in!"

Our landlord to be, Sue Black, stood near the driveway as we pulled in to check out the details. Ms. Black gathered up her small poodle, Ginger. "She won't attack you guys if you're good!" yelled out Ms. Black. After a tour of the large two-story house, we signed the paperwork and agreed to rent the house for the summer. Dan and I were working a summer temporary appointment to gain experience in order to land full-time park ranger jobs. Dan had just graduated from Clemson and I had graduated from North Carolina State. We were set for a carefree summer on the lake!

My thoughts raced at the realization of the summer ahead. We would soon be having fish fries on the back porch, riding a small paddleboat that was moored in the cove and inviting friends over for beer. Wow, this would be awesome! As Sue Black presented us with the keys to the house, she said one thing that I remember: "Hey guys, the only thing I'll mention is this is an old house and sometimes tenants hear things at night. I really think it's just because it has lots of sounds associated with rafters cooling off at night or from birds that may sometimes fly into the attic. But I don't think it will bother you guys, I bet you fellows aren't afraid of much. Ha, ha. Is that true?" We both replied that sounds in the night wouldn't even remotely be a concern. With that parting conversation, we soon were moving into the old Reed Creek farmhouse.

The Reed Creek farmhouse had a long history. We learned that it was indeed built in the Victorian period and thus over one hundred years old. We enjoyed having guests over for dinner and had several cookouts for which we invited our fellow employees over for food and beverages. Initially, the old farmhouse seemed to smile as if to exude hospitality and good times.

Then both Dan and I began to notice things. At night when we would prepare to turn in for the evening, we would hear sounds. At first the sounds resembled footsteps from an adjoining room or the upstairs area. We would also hear loud thuds that sounded like objects were being dropped from a high position. We also noticed that the longer we stayed there, the louder, more intense and more continuous the sounds became.

Then one night, after we had retired for the evening, Dan was in one room on the first floor and I was in another. Suddenly, we heard the sounds of a man screaming—what I would describe as a troubled or deranged person talking in some unintelligible format. Strangely, the voice of the man seemed to be a combination of mad laughter and broken, demonic-sounding gibberish. We could not make out the words, but the sounds continued for as much as thirty seconds or so. At the conclusion of the mumbling and moaning of the deep-voiced man, we heard a heavy crashing sound coming from the attic that sounded like a large rafter or object had fallen in. Dan and I met in the hallway simultaneously to see what was the matter. For the next couple of hours we combed the entire house looking for something or some kind of clue. We found nothing and went back to bed.

Other things began happening in the old house. Often we would awake in the morning to find that large objects had moved to other locations in the house. We noted that paintings on the wall were often moved off center so as to appear crooked or disturbed. One morning, we even found that heavy bookends consisting of old-fashioned clothing irons had been thrown from the mantel to as far as ten feet away and were lying on the floor.

One of the most bizarre happenings occurred on Halloween 1978. Dan and I invited friends over for a costume party that night. The fellowship and fun were great. Everything seemed to be fine except when the incident took place. With laughter and voices raising to loud levels from the partygoers, all at once, the party was disrupted by a large crashing sound. One of the windows on the first floor of the old house, for no apparent reason and out of nowhere, exploded before our eyes, as witnessed by about twenty-five people. Nearly everyone there that night thought the incident was supernatural. Within a few minutes the party broke up and everyone left for the evening.

Dan and I were starting to wonder what had brought all these things on and why the house seemed to have such strange and apparently paranormal events. After talking one night, we finally found a pattern that seemed to accelerate and intensify the events in the farmhouse. When we had guests over to have a party or gathering, the old Reed Creek farmhouse rebelled every time.

We later learned that the house had tragedy in its history. One of the previous owners had a problem with alcohol and some say that he drank himself to death in the old house. Things began to make sense. Dan and I thought we could see a pattern. Following what the house spirits considered a "violation of the house," it or they always reacted violently with sounds and activity. One night we even saw a fireball jump from the oven when we were heating up frozen pizza.

Finally, the fall season marked the end of our appointments as park rangers at Hartwell Lake and it was time to turn in the keys.

When we returned the keys to Ms. Black, she said one thing that startled me. "I knew you guys would eventually give up the house. No one can stay here very long. They say it's haunted."

YADKIN VALLEY ATTRACTIONS

Tourism and Travel

Blue Ridge National Heritage Area: www.blueridgeheritage.com
Caldwell County Chamber of Commerce: www.caldwellcochamber.org
Explore Wilkes: www.explorewilkes.com
North Carolina High Country: www.mountainsofnc.com
Visit North Carolina: www.visitnc.com
Wilkes Chamber of Commerce: www.wilkesnc.org
Wilkesboro Tourism Development Authority:
www.wilkescountytourism.com
Yadkin Valley Chamber of Commerce: www.yadkinvalley.org

Heritage Sites

Fort Defiance: www.fortdefiancenc.org
Overmountain Victory Trail: www.nps.gov/ovvi
Whippoorwill Academy: www.explorewilkes.com/whippoorwill.php
Wilkes Heritage Museum: www.wilkesheritagemuseum.com

OUTDOOR RECREATION

Rendezvous Mountain Educational Forest: www.ncesf.org/RMESF/home.htm
Stone Mountain State Park: www.ncparks.gov/Visit/parks/stmo/main.php
W. Kerr Scott Lake: www.saw.usace.army.mil/wkscott/index.htm
Yadkin River Greenway: www.yadkinrivergreenway.com

MUSIC EVENTS AND CONTACTS

Bluegrass in Wilkes: www.bluegrassinwilkes.com
Blue Ridge Music Hall of Fame: www.blueridgemusichalloffame.com
Carolina in the Fall: www.carolinainthefall.com
Carolina Music Ways: www.carolinamusicways.org
Merle Fest: www.merlefest.org
Wilkes Acoustic Folk Society: www.wilkesfolks.org

ARTS COUNCILS

Foothills Arts Council: www.foothillsartscouncil.org
Wilkes Art Gallery: www.wilkesartgallery.org

UPPER YADKIN AREA VINEYARDS WINERIES

Swan Creek AVA: www.swancreekvineyards.com
Yadkin AVA: www.yvwt.com

PLAYS AND MUSICALS

Wilkes Playmakers: www.wilkesplaymakers.com

Paranormal Investigations

Jeremiah Greer: www.shadowsinthedarkradio.com
jgreer@shadowsinthedarkradio.com
828.400.0836

Winston-Salem Paranormal Society:
www.meetup.com/wsparanormalsociety